Rick Sarkisian, Ph.D.

Finding Meaning
in the
7 Areas of Life
that Matter Most

LifeWork
PRESS

The contents of this book have been adapted, revised and updated from
other books written by Rick Sarkisian in order to create this single resource.

© 2007 LifeWork Press
All rights reserved.
ISBN 978-0-9743962-7-9
Library of Congress Control Number: 2005907886
Printed in the United States of America

Published 2007 by LifeWork Press, Fresno, California, USA
Distributed exclusively by Ignatius Press, San Francisco, California, USA

Cover and graphic design by Riz Marsella
Cover Photograph © Robert Llewellyn/Corbis
Illustrations by Jim Goold

DEDICATION

For all those seeking meaning and purpose in life.

Let nothing trouble you... God alone suffices.

— **Teresa of Avila**

ACKNOWLEDGMENTS

Thanks be to God for the opportunity to offer this book about meaning and purpose in life. He has placed special people in my path to guide me in the task of putting thoughts into words, starting with the always-present support of my dear wife, Cheryl. She is such an anchor for me, and my side-by-side companion.

There is also my long-time friend, Christopher Knuffke, who is so skilled in clear, spiritual thinking and amazing editorial talents that I know this book would not exist without him.

Similarly, Mark Brumley, Mike Phillips and Michael Wick have been of huge assistance in combing through various versions of the manuscript to help it become a reality in book form. Their insights and suggestions were incredibly helpful.

And to Riz Marsella, extreme gratitude for the beautiful cover design and outstanding interior layout of the book, done with superbly-drawn illustrations by Jim Goold.

Then there is my secretary, Sandy Huerta, who tirelessly and without complaint prepared one revision after another, making changes that seemed to have no end. She is a gifted woman who, beyond her skill with the printed word, has shown enthusiasm and support for this book in so many ways.

I must also acknowledge the roots in my life and profound impact made on me by my father and mother. I have been greatly influenced by the Armenian-Italian culture that was so much a part of my formative years, and what I learned about faith and family. This continues to be a source of joy in my life.

I'm also grateful for so many folks during my life who have given me experiences and encounters that now form much of the anecdotes you are about to read.

And finally, with deepest respect, let me acknowledge those "seekers" who have a yearning for truth…for meaning and direction in life… for real joy and happiness. You are on a quest that has *eternal* consequences. I pray that you will find the purpose and peace you are seeking through the *process* offered in the following pages.

CONTENTS

Introduction

THE PROBLEM

We human beings have a problem, don't we?

On the one hand, we know there's more to life than just our physical existence – yet on the other hand, for many of us, joy, satisfaction and fulfillment are elusive, no matter how hard we try to grasp them. And so we're left with a gnawing emptiness inside of us that longs to be filled.

For many people, that longing leads them from one disappointment to another, in a futile search for meaning and purpose in life. If you can identify with that problem, working with this book is a good first step toward finding the answer.

Notice I didn't say "this book will give you the answer." No book should promise you that, since every reader is on a different path, coming from different backgrounds and looking at life through different filters. There simply isn't a one-size-fits-all solution for achieving true significance in life. But if you work with this book – not just "read" it, but actively **cooperate** with the principles and challenges it provides – you'll find the answer in a rewarding, fulfilling, meaningful life.

So, when it comes to helping you find the answer to a joyful life, I can't give you a promise. But I can give you a **process**. Let's get started!

THE PROCESS

As you can see from the thickness of this book, there are many pages following this one. But don't think of them as pages – think of them as the steps of a process that will guide you from emptiness to fulfillment. A **process** of self-discovery.

Will all the steps be easy? Of course not! Few things that are worthwhile are easy. You may encounter challenges in this book that make you uncomfortable, or make you question everything you think you know about life. I want to encourage you to face those challenges head-on. Don't give up. Don't skip the hard steps. They're necessary for building a life that's filled with joy and purpose.

It's like following a recipe: many of the individual ingredients are practically flavorless, such as flour or baking powder. Others, like vinegar, are downright unsavory. But they each contribute to the overall quality of a complete, satisfying dish. Leave out the ingredients you don't like, and you'll be left with a dish that's incomplete and unsatisfying. Leave out the parts of the **process** that make you uncomfortable, and you may be left with a life that's incomplete and unsatisfying.

The primary requirement of this book is not that you **believe**, but that you are **open** to this process and put the steps of the process into **practice**. As you follow this process, you'll have the opportunity to "test" each step, learning from your own experience and setting your own pace for your journey of discovery.

So let me introduce the first step right now – the first step toward a life overflowing with meaning and satisfaction. It might be the most **difficult** challenge in the entire book. Then again, it might be the **easiest** and most natural thing for you. What is it? I'm going to ask you to **consider** that God exists.

Let me explain why: humanity is unique among all life on earth. Unlike animals, we are self-aware. We instinctively know that life has a richness and depth far beyond just our physical pleasure and fleeting happiness. Many of us spend a lifetime searching for **something** to fill the void between survival and significance. We try to fill it with power, possessions and prestige – but the emptiness remains. We want our lives to have eternal purpose and meaning – it's hard-wired into our nature – yet while everyone from philosophers to physicists has tried to solve this problem, we continue to search for an answer....

Maybe we're asking the wrong question – I believe the first and most fundamental question to ask is: "Does God exist?" I believe the emptiness we feel is a desperate need to connect with our creator.

If there's no God, then there's no answer that will truly satisfy our inner hunger for meaning in life. There's no right or wrong, no moral compass, no consequences to our thoughts, words or actions. There's only **here** and **now**. There's no hope for a better life, because this existence is all there is. Without God, then we are left only with ourselves – our own flawed human nature – and we are left to conclude that this is as good as life will ever get. Hope withers and dies, the first casualty of a godless existence.

However, **if there is a God** who created us, then we can look beyond ourselves, beyond this earthly existence, knowing that there is indeed a significant purpose for our lives.

If you can remain **open** and consider this possibility, we can continue on the steps of the process....

Did God have a reason for everything he created, from the smallest grain of sand to the largest galaxy? For creating **us**? Good question! If he did, the only way we can know that purpose is if God **reveals** it to us.

In fact, he **does** reveal his purpose.

There are two ways that God reveals himself to us: through **natural knowledge** and through **supernatural knowledge**. What's the difference?

Natural knowledge is that which we can know and understand about God by the light of **reason**. By using our intellect, we can know **that** God exists and created all things, but we can't know **why** he created us.

Supernatural knowledge is that which we can know and understand about God **only if** God reveals it to us by the light of **faith**. (Faith is **above** reason, not **against** it.) By faith, we can know not only **that** God exists and created all things, but we can also know **why** he created us. We can know his **purpose**.

So that we would discover his purpose in our lives, God reveals himself and his eternal plan to us. (We'll discuss this further in a minute.) God wants to show us the meaning of history and of our own personal lives. If we are willing to be open to God and his message, then we can find true meaning, satisfaction and joy to our lives.

The goal of this book isn't to bombard you with detailed arguments, pro and con, about God. Rather, the purpose of this book is to introduce you to a **process** that you can follow. You can test and discover the truth for yourself, and so find significance and purpose in your life. All you have to do is be open.

If you're willing to be **open** to and **consider** these things and test them for yourself – even if you're not certain, even if your worldview hasn't allowed for such beliefs until now – then I believe the rest of this book will start to make sense to you. If you already believe these things, perhaps even calling yourself a Christian, then you'll really be able to embrace what's contained in the rest of this book. So if you can begin with an open mind, you've already overcome the most significant hurdle to attaining true joy and meaning in your life.

Think of the following pages as steps in a process that will lead you to "experience" God. I believe that when you experience his presence, you'll begin to know how **real** he is. The Bible states in Ecclesiastes 3:11 that "he has put eternity into man's mind." We were created by God for eternal life, which explains our longing for something beyond this earthly life.

It is my hope and prayer that this book will help you discover that "something" – a life of true peace, joy and purpose. A life rich with meaning and significance. Life the way God intends it to be experienced!

THE PURPOSE

The search for purpose is universal among all people on planet Earth. It has led to some of our most profound thinking… and to some of humanity's most profane atrocities.

In the history of mankind, this search has ranged from simple questions to philosophy to natural religions – and, whether simple or complex, each new effort is part of humanity's continuing search for meaning and purpose in life. This search is not a dead end: there are answers to our questions. Sometimes we look to the stars above or within ourselves to fathom such answers. But, as history shows us, the answers are not written in the sky or come from within: the real answers to the big questions in life can only come from elsewhere. If we want to know God and his plan for our lives, **he must reveal it**.

Your own search may have led you through some difficult circumstances. But it's also led you to this book – which I hope will change your life forever. I pray that by the time you've closed the cover, you will **find** the purpose of your life, you will **follow** the path to understanding it, and you will embrace the plan to **fulfill** it.

First, let's explore the purpose of life itself....

THE STORY OF YOUR LIFE

In social situations, there are two kinds of people: The smooth, eloquent, charming types that can schmooze effortlessly with a winning smile. And me.

I have the ability to turn even simple conversations into memorable embarrassments… like the time I was in a local retail store and ran into a pair of important men I wanted desperately to impress – men who were in a position to refer their injury cases to me in my budding vocational rehabilitation practice. I greeted them with all the poise and professionalism I could muster, while trying to ignore a rather persistent fly that kept buzzing around my face. Maybe God wanted to shut me up, or maybe the fly was just unusually curious, but the next thing I knew the little critter had flown right into my mouth! *What should I do?* I wondered, my mind swarming with options as the fly frantically bounced from cheek to cheek in a desperate effort to escape. Finally, I reached in and grabbed it, sending the fly on its way, much to the amusement of the men I was speaking with.

Embarrassing episodes like that are the story of my life – well, at least my **social** life.

What's your story?

Have you ever thought of your life that way – as a story, a drama played out on the stage of life – filled with interesting characters and surprising plot twists? I find it helpful to view my life from this perspective, as it takes me "outside of myself" and allows me to see the bigger picture of my life and its purpose.

Of course, every story or play has an **author,** and I'd like you to consider that the **primary** author of life's story is God, revealed by his Son, Jesus Christ, as our heavenly Father. (Again, I'm only asking you to *consider* the possibility that Jesus is the Son of God.) He's writing the greatest story of all time – not just in the Bible, but throughout all of history – a living story that spans from creation to the end of time, and contains a distinct, irreplaceable role for each of us. It's the only story that really matters – the story that embraces all time, all events and all people. Including you and me.

But the Father isn't the **only** author of our lives. He's the **primary** author, since he holds the eternal plan for our lives and wants to be intimately involved with each of his characters. Through his grace, we are invited to "co-author" the story of our lives – to *collaborate* with the Father, the divine author, and so discover his will, his plan for our lives, as it unfolds day-by-day. So we are authors, too.

And, of course, every play or drama has **actors,** and I'd like you to consider that the **primary** actor in life's story is Jesus Christ. He is performing the role (or character) assigned to him by the author (the Father). In fact, he is part of the greatest story ever told. And it is our story too.

But Jesus isn't the **only** actor in our lives. He's the **primary** actor, since he has acted on our behalf by sacrificing himself on the cross for us. And through his grace, we are invited to "co-act" in the drama of our lives with him in self-giving love – to freely collaborate with Christ, the divine actor, in performing the role assigned to us – that is, to follow him in doing the Father's will in our daily lives. So we are actors, too.

Finally, every play has a **director,** and I'd like you to consider that the **primary** director in life's story is the Holy Spirit. He's directing the greatest story ever told – throughout all of time and space – guiding us to the truth of our existence and to eternal life.

But the Holy Spirit isn't the **only** director of our lives. He's the **primary** director, since he guides us to the Father's eternal plan for our lives. Through his grace, we are invited to "co-direct" the play of our lives – to collaborate with the Holy Spirit, the divine director, and so accept his guidance, fulfilling the will of the Father in the story of our lives. So we are directors, too.

"What if I don't believe all this?" Excellent question! Once again, I'm not asking you to believe this; I'm only asking you to be *open* to the possibility. Give it a shot: try it out for yourself, test if these things prove to be true, see for yourself. Then decide for yourself. Fair enough?

As actors in God's story or drama, does that mean we're locked into a pre-determined plot line that can't be changed? No. Because, unlike the traditional "cast of characters" in a play or drama – who are slaves to the whims and imagination of the author – we are actors who are free to *collaborate* in the drama – to choose, to decide, to act. Not free to determine the plot or the roles (characters), but free to be – or **not** to be – the persons God intends us to be. Free to accept or reject that God is God and we are not. Free to bring love, heroism, generosity and truthfulness to the unique roles that God has authored for us. God is able to create the story

and leave us free in our thoughts, words and actions – free to interpret the text of the author (the Father); free to follow Jesus and collaborate with him; and free to interpret the promptings of the director (the Holy Spirit).

WE LONG TO BELONG

As free characters, we can pursue happiness, joy and satisfaction however we choose. But to be truly **fulfilled** characters in God's story, we learn what it means to "belong." Everybody is born with the innate desire to belong: to a family or a friendship, to a club or a career, exercising care about who or what we belong to.

Ultimately, the choice comes down to belonging either to the world and its culture of corruption, or to God – the very author of our lives and his culture of conversion. It's our choice: it's up to us to accept or reject his grace in our lives.

Many of the characters in God's story choose to belong to the world – building on the shifting sands of power, position or pride. While on the surface these things are positive attractions, deep down they are negative addictions, and send the concept of "belonging" down a dead end street leading towards personal destruction.

But other characters choose to belong to God – building on the rock of a lifelong partnership with Christ – a *belonging* that becomes evident through their strong, satisfying relationships and through their sense of balance in the areas of life that matter most.

To belong to Christ means to belong to his family, his community – his church. Without getting bogged down in the details of theology or spirituality, we know from the Bible that Christ established the church as the family of God.

In his family, we are joined with him and belong to him. And we join the family of God by baptism. Being baptized means that we become a new person in Christ. After this, we not only belong to God's family, his community – we join with Christ and his church in regular worship. In our community worship, and in our personal reading of the Bible, we continually learn more of the true meaning and purpose of our lives. But what about all the other people and their roles (characters) in God's grand story?

They are also part of the story of our lives. In God's plan, we are not isolated individuals; we are all called to belong to God's family. We are closely interconnected to the other actors – the "cast of characters" in our lives.

They, like us, are called to collaborate with God – with the Holy Spirit directing them in fulfilling the Father's will. Every person in our lives has a different role (character) to play, yet they help us to define and fulfill our own roles. These characters – as well as the events and circumstances we encounter in the story – give relevance to our roles.

LIFE IS NOT A "DO-IT-YOURSELF PROJECT"

I want to propose that we radically change the way we view life: A change of mind and a change of heart.

Why? Because if you see yourself as the **only** author, actor and director in your story, life becomes a "do-it-yourself" project with no instructions, no sense of a master plan. It's like building your house without a blueprint. The results may leave you unfulfilled and very disappointed. The house may collapse.

But if you see yourself as part of a grand story in which you are free to collaborate with the other characters and, indeed, with the author himself, then life takes on true purpose and direction. You'll be building your house on rock (see Matthew 7:25) based on God's divine blueprint (the Bible). As a result, you'll be well on your way to ultimate fulfillment and lasting satisfaction.

If you choose to **separate yourself** from the unique, unrepeatable plan God has designed for your life, then you may never experience the joy and purpose life has to offer. It's like choosing to watch a black-and-white television with fuzzy reception and a tiny speaker, instead of a large-screen television with vivid, living color and surround sound!

There's a certain beauty – a real freedom! – in maintaining an eternal perspective. With this perspective, you can focus on things that won't pass away; and embrace those parts of your life that mean the most from God's point of view, rather than from the world's point of view. How much you love others. How consistently you live your faith. How well you are able to master your impulses and desires. We learn this eternal perspective especially in regular community worship and in daily reading of the Bible.

In his love, God created the human race, in order to share his life with us. Through sin, humanity fell away from unity with God (and one another) into division and death. To free humanity from sin, and to heal and restore us to unity – **First**, as we read in the Old Testament (Hebrew Scriptures), God promised humanity a savior and revealed his law through Moses. Through a solemn agreement (covenant), Israel accepted God's law and became the people of God. To prepare his people for salvation, God sent the prophets. **Second**, as we read in the New Testament (Christian Scriptures), God sent his Son, Jesus Christ, to fulfill his promise and save humanity from sin and restore his life in us. Through his sacrificial death on the cross and his resurrection from the dead, Christ established the new and eternal covenant between God and humanity – thus establishing the new people of God, the church.

But the Father hasn't finished his story yet, and he hasn't chiseled the plot in stone. And if we are "good" characters, accepting the Holy Spirit's guidance, we will follow Christ day-by-day in making wise and beneficial decisions, fulfilling the Father's will in our lives.

God's story is already filled with his grace – and with his truth, beauty and goodness – and the characters serve to reveal Christ's presence – his love and mercy. When, by his grace, we actively collaborate with God, the Holy Spirit will direct us in the daily decisions we make.

But what if we turn away from God, and make selfish, sinful choices? Then we can turn back to God and ask for his mercy and forgiveness. Through his Son, Jesus Christ, we can receive pardon and peace, and start afresh.

To restore and re-establish our lives in Christ, God "edits the story." He makes changes – for our own good – when we contradict God's nature and his eternal plan for us. And since his story involves a whole "cast of characters," our choices affect them as well – for better or for worse. To be a follower of Christ means to begin again, over and over… fortunately for us!

WHO DO YOU WANT TO BE?

What kind of characters will we be in God's story? That's for us to decide, based on selfishness or on the self-giving love of Jesus. We determine how we will interact with other characters, each one living out the "subplot" in which God has placed them.

Each subplot is equally worthy and important before God – whether it involves an impoverished family, a wealthy entrepreneur, a convicted criminal, a homeless veteran, a brave rescue worker, an abandoned orphan or a doting grandparent. Likewise, each **character** is equally worthy and important. Why? Because we are all equal before God – and he loves each one of us infinitely. And because Christ died for each one of us.

If we don't believe that, then our worldview narrows, elevating some characters above others. The successful executive becomes far more impressive than the relapsed drug addict. The professional athlete has greater value than a migrant farm worker. But when we see these characters from an eternal perspective, things look different....

You get the point! It all comes down to changing our perceptions **and actions,** based on divine grace and on our understanding of the author's story and our roles in Christ. It's exciting! Especially since the author doesn't show us the whole story at any one time – instead he reveals it to us gradually in the Holy Spirit and through his Word: page-by-page, chapter-by-chapter, as we journey through life – making daily, grace-filled decisions in the 7 areas of life that matter most (more on these **7 LifeWork Areas** in Part One, The Path).

OUR PERMANENT PAST

Perhaps the most daunting thing about seeing our lives as stories rather than projects is that we can no longer ignore our past. It's always right there in "black and white." Unerasable. Unchangeable. Painful events remain forever a part of the story of our lives.

But with God's help, we don't need to erase or change the past. Instead, Christ can transform the **meaning** of our past and let events remain as they were. All we need to do is ask God for his mercy and forgiveness for our past failings and sins; resolve to change by the help of his grace; and ask him to bring good out of evil. Success from failure. Healing from pain. "With God, all things are possible" (Matthew 19:26).

Then we can give our freedom to our heavenly Father. By giving him our freedom, we let him inhabit our choices – so that we act with love, honesty, courage and caring. In essence, we give our free will back to God as a gift! When we do that, we become fully involved in a story with infinite, eternal fullness – a grace-filled drama that can touch the whole "cast of characters" around us.

Giving our free will back to God as a gift – that's a radical concept that can lead us to a radically changed life!

THE PLOT THICKENS

God has given each of us the gifts of intellect and free will, which are what make us "free" characters in his story. But free to do **what?** To do anything we like, regardless of the consequences? Sadly, some people would answer "yes." But history has proven that with great freedom comes great responsibility.

So what is our responsibility to the author of the story of our lives? And what do we owe to the God who wants us to connect with him, yet allows us to make our own choices?

Let me give you my answer: I believe I owe him my very life. I want everything I do to bring glory and honor to God. I want to **belong** to him (be **where** God wants me to be – in his church), to fulfill my **vocation** in him (be **who** God wants me to be) and my **mission** in him (do **what** God wants me to do).

This, I believe, is our "LifeWork:" to accept the guidance of the Holy Spirit in using our talents, gifts, qualities, virtues and creativity; to follow Christ in every setting: home, church and world; and in this way, bring honor and glory to God, our heavenly Father. I call this approach *The LifeWork Principle*.

Our LifeWork isn't limited to choosing the right college major or career path; it's **much** more than that. Our LifeWork spans the course of our lifetime, and can be lived out in every aspect of our lives.

Just as you are different and unique from every other character in God's story, so are your personal vocation and mission, which have been custom-designed with your distinct personality and gifts in mind. By discovering your own vocation and mission, you'll have the answer to the most fundamental question you'll ever face: *what does God want me to be and do with my life?* Most people spend a lifetime pursuing that question, and unfortunately many of them look in so many wrong places, they never find the answer.

But when you *do* discover your personal vocation and mission, they can become the "roadmap" for your life's journey to the Father – with the Holy Spirit guiding you into wise decisions and virtuous actions that make your life more rewarding and purposeful. So it pays to spend time seeking your vocation and mission.

But **first,** before we go any further, a word for those of you who feel this material is going too deep for your comfort level: *relax.*

The concepts of belonging, vocation and mission can best be understood from a Christian perspective. So if you're not a Christian, these concepts may not appear to be relevant to you. But even if you don't *believe*, you can still apply them to your life – if you approach them as part of the **process** I mentioned earlier.

So the following sections do apply to you, and if you remain open, they'll help you learn more about the process of becoming the kind of person God created you to be. And that's an exciting adventure of self-discovery!

YOUR VOCATION: BEING WHO GOD WANTS YOU TO BE

God the Father has called us to a unique way of life in which He wants each of us to live a very personal vocation. Or, more accurately: **two** inter-related types of our personal vocation: general and specific.

Our **general** vocation is to live a life of holiness (self-dedication to God). God calls each one of us to personal holiness. This means more than just attending community worship; it also means daily prayer and reading of the Bible, allowing the Holy Spirit to direct us in using our unique gifts and talents, as well as maintaining purity in body, mind and spirit.

After all, God desires that our lives reveal his nature – and holiness and purity are at the very heart of God's nature. As a father, few things please me (or scare me!) more than this: hearing someone say that my children remind them of me – seeing my eyes when they look at my daughter, hearing my laugh when they joke with one of my sons. How much more must our heavenly Father want people to see his Son reflected in our lives!

Each of us also has a **specific** vocation – a unique life calling chosen by the Father, the divine author, for each character in his story. Some are called to remain single; some are called to marry; and some are called to the clergy.

Regardless of where we're coming from spiritually, we can all realize that God takes a deep interest in each one of us. And if we are open to him, he will lead us on the right path. He loves us completely, uniquely and personally, and he knows exactly the life commitment that can lead each of us to experience true joy and lasting fulfillment.

How can you know whether or not you've chosen the right vocation? Well, as with all the steps in the process, it's an ongoing journey of personal discovery.

God is speaking – are we listening? In the **Bible** and in the **signs** that God places in our lives, he speaks to us personally. And what kinds of signs are we talking about? God gives us both **external** signs (such as from family, friends and circumstances) and **internal** signs (such as peace, contentment and joy) to let us know if we're on the right track. He also allows doubt and confusion to occur, perhaps signaling that we're off track.

On the one hand, if you've ever felt that your lifestyle, career, skills and desires don't "fit together" like they should, it could be a sign that you're not in the vocation God has in mind for you. On the other hand, if you've felt a real peace about your life (not that there won't be problems and conflicts), it could mean that you're exactly where God wants you to be. Spiritual friendships and spiritual direction (faith-filled guidance from another person) will help you see and understand these signs more clearly. God may place special people in your life to help you follow his path. Look for them! Above all, ask the Holy Spirit for the grace to discover the signs he places along the path of your life journey. Trust him and follow his guidance!

YOUR MISSION: DOING WHAT GOD WANTS YOU TO DO

In addition to a personal vocation, the Father also has sent us out on a unique adventure he wants each of us to live: our personal mission. And just as with our vocation, there are two inter-related types of mission: general and specific.

Our **general** mission is to be living witnesses of Christ and his great love for us – in our thoughts, words and actions. How much does he love us? Enough to sacrifice himself on the cross for love of us, to rescue us from an eternity in hell, so that we can live for eternity in heaven in union with him.

You see, God created us to live forever with him in heaven. But almost immediately after humanity was created, we followed our free will into sin, and separated ourselves from God. No longer holy enough to be in his presence, and unable to achieve holiness through our own efforts, we created a deep chasm between ourselves and God. Not wanting to see us eternally separated from him in hell, God staged a rescue mission. He graciously sent his Son, Jesus Christ, to save us from our sins. Christ proclaimed the Good News and freely sacrificed his life for us, so that we could live eternally with God. The chasm between God and man was "bridged" – not through our own efforts, but through the life of Christ, his sacrifice on the cross and his resurrection from the dead (which paid the price for our sins and the sins of all humanity). Now, through the grace of Christ, all people can be saved and spend eternity with him in heaven. **That's** how much God loves us!

If you're a Christian, living this general mission might be the most natural and exciting part of your faith – a loving response to Christ's self-giving love. If you're not a Christian – if you're reading this because you accepted my challenge to be open and to consider that God exists – then I pray that in addition to being open, you would go beyond just "considering" and eventually come to know Jesus as Lord and Savior.

A good first step: pick up a Bible and read any of the four Gospels (Matthew, Mark, Luke or John). There you will see for yourself the unfolding mystery of God's love, mercy and salvation in Christ, who reveals the true meaning and purpose of life – in his life, death and resurrection. Each of these Gospels provides a unique portrait for you to come to a better personal knowledge and understanding of the life and mission of Jesus.

Our **specific** mission is to use our skills, virtues and spiritual gifts to honor God in everything we do. This is our "LifeWork" – to accept the guidance of the Holy Spirit in using our talents, gifts, qualities, virtues and creativity; to follow Christ in every setting: home, church and world; and in this way, to bring honor and glory to our heavenly Father. That's what it means to live *The LifeWork Principle*.

And if we belong to Christ and his family, our gifts and talents are not primarily for ourselves – God sends us to share them with our family, friends and neighbors. Just as Christ went about doing good in his life, so in him we are sent out into the world to share our time, talents and gifts. Then, through our lives, we reflect the light and love of Jesus.

Don't feel like you've got anything to give back to God? Come on, of course you do! Each and every one of us has gifts, whether few or many. Ask the Holy Spirit, and he'll direct you to the special gifts, talents and virtues *you* have already been given.

Discovering your personal vocation and mission isn't a single, once-and-for-all event. Rather, it is a gradual, yet continual "unfolding" process, sort of like an apprenticeship that never ends – and it gets better and better! – as you continually learn more about yourself and your role in God's eternal plan. Because of this, responding to God's call – striving to be and do what he wants, and becoming more like Christ – is a thread woven throughout the tapestry of your life. And accepting his call is an adventure – an adventure leading you to eternal life and happiness!

I grew up in the 1950s and '60s, when America's small screens were filled with larger-than-life heroes like Daniel Boone, Superman and Davy Crockett. But no character – real or imaginary – could top my favorite hero, "Zorro." Outfitted with his black mask, flowing cape and trusty sword, Zorro was the coolest of the cool, dashing in to save the day, week after week, on our television.

My dad, who could make just about anything, made me a fabulous sword just like Zorro's as part of my Halloween costume one year. He crafted the "blade" from a length of copper tubing, the handle from wood wrapped in black electrical tape, and a handle guard from a piece of aluminum. He even made a scabbard that hung from my belt! That Halloween, I was the envy of the neighborhood.

My father helped me conform to the image of my hero, Zorro. And today, our heavenly Father helps us conform to the image of his Son, Jesus.

And the Holy Spirit leads us to Christ and his church. Get to know Jesus in communal worship, prayer and reading the Bible. Let him become your role model. Live in him and allow him to live in you – in your daily thoughts, words and actions. In your ups and downs. In your joys and sorrows.

Allow Jesus to **transform** you and your life, so that you **reflect** him, the image and likeness of God, to others. Then you will experience for yourself true fulfillment, joy and happiness. Now and in eternity.

Part 1

THE PATH

Paths are pretty wonderful! No matter how lost you are, there's always comfort in finding a path. You may not know exactly where you're heading, but you know you'll arrive at some sort of destination – after all, no one builds a path that leads to nowhere. You may be alone, but at least you know others have traveled the path – and unless there are skeletons strewn along the way, you know they eventually got where they were going!

Paths aren't limited to parks and forests: life has many paths as well – formulas and philosophies designed to help you arrive at your destination, comforted by the fact that you're walking in other travelers' footsteps. Unfortunately, many of these paths lead to deceptively unfulfilling destinations such as financial success, physical beauty or other worldly desires, and sometimes to drugs, depression and disaster.

But Jesus has walked the paths of life and is himself the way to the Father. And his Word is a light for our path. The path to true fulfillment isn't a shortcut to superficial success; it's not a "quick fix" for life's petty problems. If you read the Bible, you come to realize: rather, the path to true fulfillment winds through every moment of every day, in every area of your life. Slowly revealing itself over the course of your lifetime: a gradual, unfolding process.

"Staying on the path" doesn't mean focusing on a single area like business or family or fitness. It means focusing on Christ, on your vocation and mission in him, where you will find the right balance in all of the important areas of your life – and so discover the key to a life that's rewarding in every way.

❧ THE 7 LifeWork Areas ❧

I heard the story of a man who was ordering a pizza, when the waitress asked if he'd like it cut into eight slices or twelve. He replied, "Better make it eight... I don't think I could eat twelve."

Aren't you and I a lot like that man? And life is a lot like that pizza: it's going to fill your days no matter how you slice it. For some people, life has only two "slices" – work and family. Others go to the opposite extreme, breaking life into several – even dozens – of "slices." Neither view is particularly helpful in terms of achieving a **balanced** life; one's too vague, the other's too detailed. What's the solution?

For the purposes of our discussion, I believe life can be "sliced" into seven areas that matter most. (And yes, I realize this is where the pizza analogy falls apart. Ask for your next pizza to be cut into seven slices and see what kind of look you get from your waiter!) Each day, we consciously or unconsciously allocate our time to these seven areas; each day different from the one before. I call them the **7 LifeWork Areas,** which we'll soon explore in detail. For now, on the next page, is an overview:

	1	FAITH	Believing that God is active in every aspect of the story of your life.
	2	RELATIONSHIPS	Appreciating your own story as well as creatively collaborating with God and the "cast of characters" you encounter in your story.
	3	WORK	Understanding how the Father has *equipped* you for your story and *sent* you out in a specific role to accomplish your work. And then doing it.
	4	KNOWLEDGE	Learning how you and your role fits into the grand story of life.
	5	SOCIETY	Helping others, the "cast of characters," as your story unfolds.
	6	FITNESS	Keeping yourself strong and healthy in body, mind and spirit.
	7	LEISURE	Regularly slowing down the pace of your story to give yourself rest and relaxation.

❧ HOW DO I FIND MEANING IN LIFE?

Most aspects of your life will fit into one of these **7 LifeWork Areas**. Likewise, each of the **7 LifeWork Areas** are present in a well-balanced life. And that is the key: balance.

Think of it this way: imagine that every morning, you wake up and find on your breakfast table a full pitcher of water and seven empty cups – one for each of the key areas of life. The pitcher of water represents the amount of time in one day of your life, so every drop of water is poured out into the seven cups. How do your cups look? Are some **overflowing**, while others are **empty?** That's the sign of an unbalanced life. Don't worry – it's a very common situation, but it also needs your immediate attention.

Many of us tend to pour much of our time into **work**. Which means the other key areas of life only get the meager leftovers: a couple of ounces for **faith** and perhaps a dribble of **leisure.** Some areas go empty altogether....

If you're a student, perhaps you fill your **knowledge** cup every day, with maybe a little splash into **leisure** and perhaps a few drops into **relationships** or **fitness**. Here again, some important life areas have received none of your time.

When a cup overflows, all the spilled water is wasted. You can't recapture it. It's the same with time. Whatever time you waste can never be recovered – you either use it well in the seven specific **LifeWork Areas,** or use it poorly and waste it away.

It's all about *balance*, which means making sure that you devote time to all of the **7 LifeWork Areas**, in the context of your personal vocation and mission... and not focusing on some areas at the expense of others. It is an opportunity to apply *The LifeWork Principle* in every aspect of your life.

Chapter 1

FAITH

Pursuing my passion for pre-war Fords often drew me to old car swap meets, a veritable feast for those looking for parts to complete their auto restoration projects. Usually staged in large outdoor venues like fairgrounds, these swap meets offer acres and acres of rusty fenders, flywheels and other body parts, always more junk than jewels. All browsed by hundreds of glassy-eyed men walking through the sea of discards as if in a daze, overwhelmed by the endless panorama of "stuff."

These auto parts are the discards of the material world. A wheel from an old Packard. A carburetor for a Studebaker Six. Door handles for a 1941 Chevrolet. Rusty, rotting, recycled or reproduced. It's all there.

What a stark reminder of how the things of this world pass away, but the things of God – love, joy, peace and truth – never pass away. Which makes our choice obvious: we can place our confidence in the world's junkyard of possessions, power and position, or we can place our confidence in God, and seek out those events, experiences and encounters that have *eternal* consequences. It's up to us – it's our choice.

But how can we know that God is **real**?

Even longtime Christians struggle with this question from time to time. One way is to look for the signs and clues he has given us. God is alive, active and enmeshed in our day-to-day existence. We can accept this at face value, just as we can accept the contents of a soup can by reading the label. We don't need to open it to know that there's chicken broth inside. The label tells us so. In a similar way, God has left us an abundance of "labels" – especially in the Bible! – as well as historical events, men and women who lived and died for their faith... all this and more, so that we can believe with confidence in the one who made us.

Our faith is a gift from God. At the same time, faith is like a seed. When properly nurtured, the seed grows into something big and beautiful, something fruitful. On the other hand, if the seed is ignored or abused, it will never blossom into maturity. Reading Scripture and praying, alone and in community worship, are excellent ways to grow the seed of faith.

Prayer especially is a powerful tool: our daily spiritual walk is an opportunity for **constant** prayer, not just prayer once a day or when we "feel" like it. We can pray while walking, driving or riding in planes, buses or elevators. We don't need formal prayers – we can just acknowledge God's presence, and invite him into the moments of our lives.

It's a decision either to actively seek God each day or to passively keep him in the shadows of your life. If you decide to actively seek him, this requires a **commitment** to know, love and serve him wherever you find yourself: at home, at work or in the world.

It is a matter of **choosing** whether to fully embrace Christ's lordship over your whole life or to merely keep him in your back pocket as a "concept." It's a choice between regularly talking with him in daily moments of prayer (conversation with God), or just giving him the leftovers (brief acknowledgement) once the day's events are concluded.

■ WHY BE QUIET?

Silence is the classroom of prayer. It is a place where God often speaks to our hearts – perhaps because we aren't talking so much. He commands us in the Bible to "Be still, and know that I am God" (Psalm 46:10). It may well be that he gave us two ears and one mouth in direct proportion to the way he wants us to use them!

Listening to God allows us to experience the prompting of the Holy Spirit, that "inner voice" in our heart, given to each person who asks Jesus to be the Lord of their life. The Holy Spirit tells us – sometimes directly, sometimes subtly – whether we are doing right or wrong. When we belong to Christ and his family, the Holy Spirit inhabits our conscience and directs us in our daily life. When we are on the right track, there is a sense of peace, comfort and a "good fit" (like putting on a favorite pair of comfortable shoes). A strong conscience identifies what is truly good and truly evil. Those with a weak conscience have difficulty telling the difference.

When we get off track, the Holy Spirit allows feelings of confusion, even guilt – letting us know we're not making the right choices. When we live this kind of "off track" lifestyle, we're basically following our selfish inclinations, which separates us from God and his grace. The by-products are often feelings of sorrow and anxiety. These feelings may encourage us to return to God and get back on the right track.

How do we allow ourselves to wander off course? Often it's by yielding to temptation – which seems to be everywhere, flowing from the world, the flesh, the devil... the usual suspects. Temptation (darkness leading us to sin) is the opposite of inspiration (light leading us to holiness). We are fooled into thinking we can **flirt** with temptation – just "checking it out" – without actually **crossing the threshold** into sin. But it doesn't stop there, does it? Christ knows our frailty, and encourages us in the Bible to "watch and pray that you may not enter into temptation" (Matthew 26:41).

So, allow silence and solitude to be the "classroom" of your prayer life. Let quiet moments connect you more strongly to God's Word and to the guidance of the Holy Spirit. In times of doubt or crisis, listen to that "still, small voice" of the Holy Spirit and you will know what to do. Then, as the saying goes, "just do it!"

■ Is God on your schedule?

Beyond spending daily moments with God as events around us unfold, set aside a specific time and place for entering into prayer. Make it the **same** time and place each day, if possible. Protect and use this time as a way to go to the fountain to be refreshed by God's Word, grace and guidance.

For me, my "appointment with God" is scheduled each morning on a jogging path or the treadmill at the gym. As I gear up for my workout, I enter into my private conversation with God – a conversation that can include praise, thanksgiving, repentance, requests and resolutions. I even use foam earplugs to tune out the sounds and music that fills the gym environment.

The world has many "broadcasts" that battle for our attention: entertainment, titillation, gossip, raunchy humor and more. It's impossible to listen to God if you're tuned into the world; it's like trying to listen to AM and FM radio simultaneously. Doesn't work! Praying effectively requires us to *tune out* the world's broadcasts, so that we can *tune in* the clear message of God's Word and then speak with him in the silence of our hearts.

■ How do you measure time?

We often are obsessed with the clock: *"What did I accomplish in my 10-hour workday? Does the clock tell me I'm industrious or lazy?"* We allow the clock to be our judge and jury, making us feel good or bad about how we use time. We think of time as just another resource – something to be managed, parceled out and applied to our tasks. We read books about "time management" to help us better prioritize our day. But we can view time differently.

Time is truly a gift from God – the gift of life itself! It needs to be sanctified, made holy in Christ. With the help of God's grace, we can learn to use time to make the moments of our life opportunities to grow in holiness.

For example, when you experience times of struggle or sadness, connect with God by laying your burdens before him. Ask for his help – after all, he is our Father. This parent-child relationship is perhaps best seen in the way his own Son, Jesus, addressed God as "Abba," which is best translated as "Daddy" (see Mark 14:36). Christ's relationship with the Father was incredibly intimate. Is **yours?**

As you rethink the importance of time, consider this:
To know TIME is to know BALANCE.
To know BALANCE is to know PEACE.
To know PEACE is to know GOD.
To know GOD is to know JOY.

Whenever we try to **dominate** time or **disregard** it altogether, we're taking a worldly view of time. Instead, think of time as a remarkable **gift** from God – a **treasure** entrusted to us. What a privilege! And what a responsibility.

While we can never repay God for making us stewards of his gift of time, we have the opportunity to "give our time back to God" as we present our lives to him at death. All we have done throughout our lives, our LifeWork, will be laid before our heavenly Father, as we leave the realm of time and enter eternity. And are we preparing for him to see how we allowed the Holy Spirit to direct us in doing the Father's will… in following Christ… during the time he entrusted to us?

■ WHAT'S SO AMAZING ABOUT GRACE?

To experience divine grace is to know the peace and joy that can only come from God. What is "grace?" It is the favor, the free and undeserved help that God gives us in Christ to respond to his personal call to become his children. Grace is our participation in God's own life. Grace is spiritual food to nourish us on our journey through life, to be gained or lost by how we choose to live. It's your choice to accept it or reject it. It's always offered.

The more we know God and surrender our lives to him, the greater our capacity to hold whatever graces we receive. We become like an ever-expanding vessel, as we grow in our capacity to know, love and serve him. When we have divine grace in our life, we experience true joy – which is so much better, different and long-lasting than the passing experience of "happiness" – which depends on something "happening" in a desired way, otherwise we are "unhappy." (Notice there is no such word as "unjoy.")

As I said before, sin separates us from God and deprives us of his grace. Just as certainly as God exists, so too does his enemy, Satan. This fallen angel, who the Bible calls the "father of lies" (see John 8:44), has tremendous power and influence over the world in which we live – and he proves it by constantly placing doubts and temptations across our path. When we stumble and fall through our own choice, we lose God's grace, while Satan gains a victory. Satan wants us to feel ashamed, guilt-ridden, angry and resentful, **permanently**. He does not want us to repent, ask forgiveness or start over. God wants to bring us back to himself and his grace.

How can we restore our relationship with God after stumbling into one of Satan's traps? **We** can't. But **God** can – through forgiveness, giving us pardon and peace through his Son, Jesus Christ. When we confess our failings to God, ask him to forgive us and to help us turn away from our sins, he will wipe the slate clean! We don't deserve forgiveness, and certainly can't earn it on our own merits (by being "good") – it is only given to us by the grace of Christ, won for us by his sacrifice on the cross. Of course, we can start afresh, with firm resolutions to avoid sin and follow Christ in our lives.

■ CAN HOUSEWORK BE HOLY?

We can be extraordinary in ordinary things – in the everyday events, tasks and settings that surround us – such as doing housework, shopping for groceries, cutting the lawn, washing the car, folding clothes, making dinner, working and going to school. These are all personal opportunities for holiness and grace-filled moments, and for listening to the quiet voice of the Holy Spirit within our hearts. But it is up to us to **recognize** these opportunities and **act** on them.

In today's culture of activity and accumulation, we all have too much clutter, too many distractions. We allow ourselves to be overbooked, overcommitted and overrun with possessions. But it is often in the simplicity and ordinary events that we find the majesty and mystery of God at work in our lives. Ever sense that presence of God while in the mountains, or at the ocean, far from our normal surroundings?

What God has given to us, we can share with those around us: our time, our talents and skills, our money and possessions. Give and give freely. Give abundantly.

In every moment and every circumstance, seek the Father's will, what He calls you to do – in thought, word or action – as an expression of your love for him. Let the Holy Spirit direct you to make wise choices. And live according to your choices, inspired and strengthened by daily prayer and reading of the Bible.

■ Is your faith overflowing?

Faith is the most important area of our lives because it involves our relationship with both God and our neighbor. It is priority #1. As such, it has a **dual** role in the 7 LifeWork Areas. Faith is both a stand-alone **LifeWork Area** and an integral aspect of all the other **LifeWork Areas.** Faith can permeate **all** that we do over the course of our lives. This faith enlightens us about the true meaning and purpose of our lives.

> Faith can permeate all that we do over the course of our lives.

Faith is a gift. And the gift becomes our task. While faith is a gift freely offered by God, it is also something that can be prepared for, fostered and expanded through studying Scripture, reading good spiritual books, reflecting on our life and searching for meaning.

God wants just one thing from each of us: **everything**. He wants us to be completely Christ's – to surrender our lives to him and, by so doing, to experience the kind of peace, joy and freedom that comes about by living the spiritual life. Guided by the Holy Spirit, it is a **collaborative partnership in** which, side-by-side, we follow him day-by-day, on our journey to our Father in heaven.

I have often told each of my kids, "If you're called to the vocation of marriage, make sure to find a spouse who puts God first in their life. You don't want to be first; you want God to be first for yourself and your mate." That's the grounding in **faith** that anchors us through the ups and downs of married life and any other calling we may have.

Chapter 2

RELATIONSHIPS

The old, beat-up van in front of me had some writing on the back doors. A Bible verse, I assumed – something that would no doubt enhance my spiritual life through a freeway encounter pre-arranged by God himself! I increased my speed so that I could pull closer to the van and read the passage.

As it turned out, the writing wasn't a Scripture verse. But it did have meaning for me… and still does. The message read:

NOT YOUR WAY

NOT MY WAY

BUT YAHWEH

(In the Old Testament, God's name is Yahweh [or sometimes translated Jahveh or Jehovah], which means "God Saves.")

In other words, **God's way.** Not "have it your way" or "I did it my way." It reminded me that following God's plan needs to be our focus, rather than the plans we concoct for ourselves or those we adopt from the influence of others. I once heard it said: "If you want to give God a good laugh, tell him your plans!"

In order to have meaningful relationships, we can strive to understand the God-given plans held by others in our lives. Besides seeking the unique map God has drawn for our own lives, we can also seek the maps he has developed for those we love and care for. The more we get to know one another's maps, the more satisfying our relationships will be.

If we can view all others as equally important "drivers" in the journey of our lives, then we enhance our ability to grow in key virtues like love, humility and respect. Rather than viewing ourselves as the center of the universe, we view ourselves as motorists sharing the road with others who are following God's map for their lives. That makes us accountable to him for all that we think, say and do for touching the hearts and minds of others.

Our aim in life takes on eternal meaning because our actions affect others and affect how we proceed in the road trip of life. Like a vehicle's navigation system, the Holy Spirit guides our conscience along the way. We just need to listen and accept his guidance in our daily life.

> The more we get to know one another's maps, the more satisfying our relationships will be.

If we are driven in the direction of power, prestige and possessions, then we are moving toward a worldly destination that is ever-elusive and only involves others to the extent that we gain from the interaction.

On the other hand, if we steer ourselves in the direction of humility, respect and love for others as we make the journey God has mapped out for us, then we experience the ever-present goodness and fruitfulness of his grace. God nurtures our sense of belonging as we live out the biblical command to "bear one another's burdens" (Galatians 6:2). The effects of these relationships extend far beyond our circle of family and friends, allowing the light of Christ's love to penetrate the dark and despairing world around us.

That means each of our relationships are not only filled with positive regard and respect for others, but also contribute to their well-being and personal needs.

If your relationships with others need improvement, then pray that God will provide you with the tools (virtues) you need to become a better spouse, parent, friend or relative. Then accept the tools and get to work!

❧ HOW CAN I HAVE MEANINGFUL RELATIONSHIPS?

Through your acts of kindness and thoughtfulness, Jesus can reach the hearts and souls of others in powerful ways. From an eternal perspective, these actions are your personal way of following Christ, rather than a quest for selfish outcomes and rewards. Don't worry about results. After all, many of our good actions simply plant seeds in the lives of others and God takes it from there. Mother Teresa of Calcutta spoke about the importance of being *faithful* rather than successful. So keep your eye on the *root* and not on the fruit.

If you want to change the landscape of the relationships that surround you, first decide how important it is to do so. Ask yourself: what drives me now in my relationships? Selfishness or the self-giving love of Christ? How do I view other people? Do I want to have more solid and lasting relationships? What needs to change most in me?

It's all about change. It is a decision to reach out in love to those around you – cutting loose of your brokenness, your past disappointments, your lingering hurt and anger and your emotional baggage.

The alternative is to remain where you are, spinning your wheels and making no forward progress in how you talk, act and think, and in the way you treat others. I pray that you won't let that happen. Instead, view **every single person** as God's created wonder <u>and</u> as a fellow traveler. Part of the "cast of characters" in life's story.

ASK the Holy Spirit for the grace to know what you should do to help others.

SEEK improved relationships with difficult or unpleasant people. It shouldn't be hard to find them – they're everywhere, even in our own families.

OFFER help to others in need, whether you're asked to or not. Expand your view of the word "need" to include not just those with physical needs like shelter, food or clothing, but also those with emotional, moral or spiritual needs.

PRAY daily for the needs of others. God loves it when you do so, and those around you will truly feel the impact of your prayers.

Actions result in reactions. When you start to change the way you view others, then you ignite exciting new dimensions and greater depth in those you encounter. Not just those close to you, but even casual or coincidental relationships.

The payoff is a refreshing, grace-filled view of life from above "ground zero" and toward an eternal perspective that points you and others toward God's eternal kingdom.

■ WHO'S WATCHING YOUR KIDS?

> ## AS PARENTS, MAKE IT YOUR PRIORITY TO:
>
> - PROTECT them from spiritual, emotional and physical harm.
> - EQUIP them with the tools and skills necessary for adulthood.
> - GUIDE them in making wise LifeWork choices.
> - TEACH them authentic manhood and womanhood.
>
> > WARNING: Failure to practice the above formula allows the world, in all its superficiality and corruption, to practice it for you!

Our kids are only young and impressionable for a short time, so this is the opportunity of a lifetime.

Driving along the freeway one morning, I was thinking about some news that my wife had just given me: she was pregnant with our fifth child. I began to "do the math" and realized that I would be 48 at her birth, 65 when she finished high school and over 70 when she finished college. None of those numbers put a smile on my face, and I realized why – I was thinking about myself rather than the special gift he had given us! I was ashamed, and knew that I should be humbled before God – knowing that in his mysterious ways, he felt my wife and I were actually *worthy* to raise another of his precious souls. There was an immediate shift in my thinking, and I became thankful and at peace with God's providence. I put away my mental calculator and started smiling.

■ WHAT ARE FRIENDS FOR?

Seek the company of those who are "driving in your direction" on life's road trip, regardless of where they are on their journey. Find those who seek goodness in life, and share your faith with them. As it says in the Bible "iron sharpens iron" (Proverbs 27:17).

❧ How do I practice patience and humility?

We are not alone on this journey. We have the opportunity to establish spiritual friendships for accompaniment as we travel through the twists and turns common to our existence. A spiritual friendship is based on finding common ground in matters of faith, seeking to understand the vocation, mission and life-purpose of our fellow travelers. As we do so, we accept where they are on the spiritual journey, rather than trying to diagnose where they ought to be. These relationships can extend beyond those with whom we are comfortable, and we can reach out to the poor, lonely, rejected, unapproachable or angry people that exist in every community. Extend the hand of friendship, illuminated by faith.

■ What's so virtuous about patience and humility?

Make this your priority list: God first, others second, yourself third. You might even say, "God first, second *and* third" because he is needed in our relationships with others as well as in our own personal lives.

Living in an agricultural area of California affords my family many unique opportunities, not the least of which is finding our way through the annual "corn maze" each October. Take a few acres of tall cornstalks, plow out a maze with lots of twists, turns and dead ends, and you've got a corn maze. The secret to navigating the corn maze? Patience and being humble enough to ask for outside help from strategically-positioned "corn cops." (I've been trapped with my daughter in the corn maze for two hours into the dark of night until "rescued" by one of these aides!)

Other than sleeping, our waking moments are filled with daily circumstances and people that provide opportunities to display patience and humility. And the more you demonstrate these virtues, the more you stay on course and reflect the image of God.

Is it easy? No. Practicing patience and humility is like practicing physical exercise – it's challenging but effective. The more challenging the exercise, the stronger you become. So we can commit ourselves every day to growing in these vital human virtues (see the separate chapters on Patience and Humility in Part 2, THE PATTERN).

■ WHO NEEDS YOUR HELP RIGHT NOW?

Look for opportunities to guide and counsel others, especially teenagers and young adults. Honor them with your kindness and find at least one person you can help. Being consistently kind means overcoming our self-centeredness and exercising thoughtfulness, understanding, compassion and good deeds.

Want to find real peace in your heart? Consider the bookmark of Mother Teresa, which she often called her "business card:"

The fruit of Silence is

PRAYER

The fruit of Prayer is

FAITH

The fruit of Faith is

LOVE

The fruit of Love is

SERVICE

The fruit of Service is

PEACE

Mother Teresa

While others may not always bring us a sense of peace, we will find peace if our relationships are based on a servant's heart, rooted in Christ.

Think of other people as daily, living opportunities to practice the virtues most important in our lives – the virtues of Christ. In the process, we will learn more about God and ourselves. We'll see areas that could stand improvement in the way we interact with others and we will also see improvements in growing into the image and likeness of Jesus.

■ HAD ANY SENIOR MOMENTS LATELY?

Connect with the elderly, not just those in your family, but also those forgotten in rest homes and convalescent hospitals. Tap into their wisdom and life experiences. We have much to learn by their trials, failings and successes. Plus, we are given a rich heritage of times past, of simpler living in a world far less frenetic than today.

> We will find peace if our relationships are based on a servant's heart.

It's important to show patience, especially with the elderly that you have in your own family. Sometimes the elderly require as much (if not more) patience than what we show our own children. The fruits of practicing the virtue of patience include less volatility in our relationships, less stress in our lives and a greater sense of self-control. It's a way for keeping tension at bay. At both extremes, from the very young to the very old, patience and calmness allow us to reflect the light of Christ and his love to others.

■ WASTING TIME IS A GOOD THING?

Yes, I'm actually **encouraging** you to waste a little time… with a friend. Sometimes the best mark of a good friend is someone you can just hang out with, needing no particular purpose or event or agenda. Don't forget family members!

And "wasting" time really isn't "wasting" anything. It is using the gift of time in an uncluttered, unscheduled, spontaneous and creative way. Sometimes in these

❧ HOW DO I SIMPLIFY MY LIFE?

moments, we discover God's presence in the simple, ordinary aspects of life. Simple is good!

Do you remember the simplicity of your childhood? I certainly do. Yo-yos, bicycles and baseballs. Comic books, western movies, marbles and black-and-white television. Simple joys that I still fondly remember (and occasionally long for) all these years later.

It's the simple slices of life that are well-remembered and well-used. They shape who we are, and forecast who we will become. If we latch on to the simple, the common, the ordinary that fills each day, then we can grow in our faith and devote ourselves to the things that matter most.

Seek the uncomplicated, the "user-friendly." It's the complex that demands daily attention from us, often to the point of distraction. Switching to as many simple interests, events and connections as possible will do much to let us enjoy the free, unscheduled time we have available (or make available).

Chapter 3

WORK

The first car I owned was a fairly uninspiring green 1951 Chevrolet sedan. But when I sold it to purchase my second car, I was elevated into a position of prestige and prominence among my peers, for I was the proud owner of a 1957 Chevrolet 2-door hardtop. In tropical turquoise, no less!

But the initial monetary outlay was only the beginning of my investment in the Chevy. I spent the next two years striving to "improve" a car that was generally considered to be top-of-the-line to begin with. I spent money on everything from a tachometer to traction bars, custom wheels to a Corvette engine. The more items I bought, the more items I felt the car needed. My '57 Chevy soon became a money pit on wheels.

Ultimately, I sold the car. It never ran all that well anyway. It overheated, idled roughly, often stalled, and rode like a tractor. No seller's remorse here – it was gone and good riddance. But I learned a valuable lesson.

I realized that if you mess too much with the factory-engineered original, you change the intent of the design and the architecture of something made to work well as-is.

In the world of work, we are also designed to function in the way God created us, using our talents to fulfill his mission for us in this life. When we try to change that design and "reinvent" ourselves – an act of futility! – we tamper with the original work of God's Design and Engineering Department.

When we think of work, we usually think of our job, career or profession. Many of us use our work to define who we are. It's common to ask a new acquaintance, "What do you do?" As if that were the person's identity. Yet work as a single focus limits the possibilities for using our gifts and talents in the broader sense. Remember, work is just **one** part of our LifeWork, which involves **all** that we do with all we are given in the settings in which we find ourselves.

> Consider work as a daily expression of our love for God and our neighbor.

So let's change the way we look at work: Rather than seeing work as a means of our economic gain (or sometimes survival), let's consider work as a daily expression of our love for God and our neighbor.

■ HOW CAN YOU CHANGE YOUR VIEW OF WORK?

By acknowledging that all you have to offer the working world comes from God – your abilities, brainpower and physical competence. And his gift becomes your task: You offer him your love and thanks by being a productive, dependable and competent worker in your chosen profession. When you use your skills with this mindset, others see God's presence in the way you conduct yourself.

In effect, your work becomes a daily "thank you" to the one who equipped you with the talents, gifts and abilities that enable you to work in the first place!

If you believe that God has not only given you certain abilities, but also wants you to use them in a particular way, then keep reading. This book is definitely for you. If it's difficult to believe this, then you may face the lifelong challenge of trying to figure out the answers to life through the dice-roll of accidents and coincidences. In other words, you're on your own!

A BETTER UNDERSTANDING OF YOUR ROLE IN THE WORKPLACE COMES FROM ACKNOWLEDGING THAT:

- All you have comes from God.

- He has a plan for your life.

- He wants you to use your skills and abilities wisely in all **7 LifeWork Areas.**

- Work, in and of itself, can express the love and gratitude you have for God.

Sharpen your new perspective by placing yourself in settings that make the most use of your skills, and "think bigger than your job" so that you can see daily opportunities to apply your talents across all **7 LifeWork Areas.**

Do this, and you'll become a dynamic, living example of who God made you to be. And you'll be a tremendous inspiration to those around you, who will see how you live out God's call in every setting in which you find yourself.

Just as exciting, the landscape that surrounds your life will gradually begin to change. Like a painting of the countryside, there will be more than the farmer's house in the picture. There will also be rolling hills, vineyards, expansive sky, and so many more details that would otherwise be hidden from view. The world around you will seem broader and larger than you noticed before.

This is because you will have established a creative partnership with God. Your capacity to embrace life increases, and you realize that the narrow focus on "job" or "career" is limiting, compared with the wide-angle view of how you become involved in the **7 LifeWork Areas.**

More than ever, you'll see how your life and your life's work fit into God's map for your journey. You'll dramatically improve your use of time, seeing it as a precious gift from the one who created it. The moments of the day will flow by with a greater sense of calling, mission and purpose – so that whatever you do (or don't do) becomes a matter of creative collaboration in the role God has specifically set aside for you in this world!

■ WHAT DOES WORK HAVE TO DO WITH LOVE?

Since your skills, talents and gifts come from God, then work is the perfect place to apply them and apply them well. By doing so, you express your love and gratitude to both God and your neighbor.

Work also means sacrifice, applying your abilities to tasks that are required in your home, your job and the community in which you live. This takes our time – time that could be used for other pursuits unrelated to work, such as leisure and recreation. But when we give of ourselves sacrificially in performing work of any sort, we are expressing our love – authentic love for those we support, for our employers, for God himself. In this, we can imitate the self-giving love of Jesus, who sacrificed himself for us and our salvation.

Warning! For some, self-identity is defined by one's work. Yet what you do in work does not equal who you are. In reality, **who** you are depends on **whose** you are. Your identity is truly defined by your relationship with God, by belonging to Christ and his family, the church. By all you do in the **7 LifeWork Areas**.

■ HAVE YOU PUT OFF KICKING THE PROCRASTINATION HABIT?

Doing nothing can be a good thing, especially if it is a time for rest, recovery or reflection. But routinely doing nothing when there are projects that need completing is a sign that you aren't using your time wisely or well. That's procrastination – a typical response to tasks that are boring, unpleasant, difficult or confusing – and it results in tasks being put off for no good reason. When trying to use the gift of time in wise and holy ways, remember: procrastination is public enemy #1.

Conquering procrastination isn't easy. After all, it requires changing "circuitry" that's probably been in place for a long time. Changing the "wires" takes more than just time management books. It takes your personal commitment to getting the job done without delay. And, above all, it takes **action**.

The most effective people are often those who are willing to perform difficult or unpleasant tasks – the things that no one else wants to do. They overcome any internal resistance and do what needs to be done. They are "doers," not "stewers." Are you a "doer?"

Overcoming procrastination is important for self-mastery and makes us powerful role models for our children. By example, we can teach them the importance of work, of getting things done without complaint or delay, of work as a form of sacrifice, of self-giving love. We live in a culture that avoids sacrifice and flees suffering of any sort – yet both conditions, while unpleasant, can transport us to a deeper, more intense relationship with God.

■ **WHAT DO YOU HAVE TO OFFER?**

Sharing our personal qualities with people in need is another meaningful way to add greater depth to our lives. Life once again becomes bigger when we help others in need of food, clothing, shelter, cash, emotional support or spiritual comfort.

As Christ himself observed, "The harvest is plentiful, but the laborers are few" (Matthew 9:37). Go into the vineyard of life and enjoy the satisfaction of helping others less fortunate than you. Give something back to your community as a way of saying thanks to God.

You say this sounds daunting? Then you're probably thinking that you'll have to make a major commitment or tackle some huge undertaking. **Don't**. Start **small**. Build slowly. That's how all good habits become imbedded in our lives. After all, we're building new circuitry into our brains!

Seek at least one opportunity to volunteer your time in the next thirty days, and then stay with it. There are plenty of options to choose from, in your church, homeless shelters, food banks, handicapped settings, homes for the elderly and hospitals for children or adults.

Clearly, volunteering is an outstanding way to practice and grow in the important virtues of love, humility and kindness. Taking free time and filling it in with the joy of helping others allows the light of Christ to reflect through you – to shine as an example of one who serves God's people. Like Father, like Son. Like Son, like servant. In doing this we will come to be like Jesus, who came "not to be served, but to serve" (Mark 10:45).

■ WANT TO ORGANIZE YOUR TIME, BUT CAN'T FIND ANY?

Are you scattered and disorganized, zig-zagging from one activity to another just to get through it all? If so, then consider a simple and time-proven solution to the chaos and confusion that accompanies such days:

> # Take time each day to plan the next.

Spend just five to ten minutes each evening planning the next day. Take more time if you need to. Write down what you'll do and when you'll do it. Then prioritize the list, in order of importance. Let this serve as your daily "personal trainer." But try not to plan your free time, even if you have lots of leisure activities in mind for a day off. It's easy to overdo it so that a free day becomes just another workday.

In other matters, such as dealing with clutter, saving too many items or surrounding yourself with too many possessions, begin using the trash can or give-away box aggressively to simplify, simplify, simplify. The less you have, the less you have to worry about. Less really **is** more! Clean out your closet. Think about it: how many shirts, shoes, suits and sweaters do you really need? Especially when the need for clothing is so great among the world's poor.

In the long term, identify the important things you want to accomplish. Set specific, written goals for yourself, especially for each of the **7 LifeWork Areas** (use the **LifeWork Action Plan Grid** on pages 144-145). Create an integrated relationship between short-term and long-term goals, so that what you do in the near future helps you make progress toward the goals you've set for the distant

❧ How can I avoid burnout?

future. For example, if your long-term goal is to open a food and clothing storage facility for the poor, begin by volunteering in a homeless shelter or social service agency to gain first-hand experience. Then you'll have a foundation you can build on for the long term.

■ ARE YOU HEADING FOR BALANCE OR BURNOUT?

The theme song of the workaholic includes at least one verse that praises "work for the sake of work" and a refrain that asks repeatedly: "what are you avoiding?" These are tough issues that can be faced head-on in order to properly ease out of the overload/overwork syndrome.

Remember the analogy of the pitcher of water (time) and the seven cups (**7 LifeWork Areas**)? Which of your cups are overflowing right now? Which remain empty? How can you more evenly distribute the water that sustains you each day? If you are working too much, try pouring some water into the cups labeled **Relationships**, **Fitness** and **Leisure**.

Balance helps to avoid burnout in any of the **7 LifeWork Areas**, but perhaps most often in the area of work. Too much of our time spent in one area causes neglect in other areas, and affords little margin or free time between them. When we are overworked, overloaded and overcommitted we find a decline in quality, enthusiasm and interest.

Burnout occurs not only in activities, but also in the proliferation of information. Some refer to this as "information overload," although I believe most of what streams our way each day might better be termed "non-information overload." So much data flows through our lives that no one person can analyze or assimilate it all. To avoid burnout, try not to absorb every piece of data you encounter. Learn how to skim through the fluff to find the important information. You'll help keep your life in balance. And balance is the antidote for burnout.

7 WAYS TO IMPROVE THE QUALITY OF WORK:

- SEEK balance in life.

- CONQUER procrastination.

- PLAN and ORGANIZE daily.

- APPLY skills and gifts competently and well.

- SEE work as **part** of a satisfying life, rather than its **source** of satisfaction.

- REMEMBER that work = love, **not** work = money.

- DEVELOP a real sense of mission and purpose in life.

Chapter 4

KNOWLEDGE

In addition to being a self-proclaimed car nut, I have another confession to make: I **love** tools. There's just something about having workshop drawers filled with wrenches, sockets, pliers and power tools... pegboards hung with mallets, hammers, files, saws and clamps... and, of course, roll after roll of duct tape. What workshop would be complete without it?

Each tool was designed to perform a particular function. As I learned in high school auto shop, there's always a "right tool for the right job." You can't change a spark plug with a tire iron and you can't drill holes with a socket wrench. So, **knowledge** of tools and how they work is as important as the actual **skill** in using them.

Think of Christ as the "Master Craftsman" who has a limitless supply of tools for getting us through life. Tools for maintenance, breakdowns and repairs. Tools for raising children. Tools for the working world. Tools for the spiritual journey. Even tools to mend broken hearts.

God freely gives us all the tools we need. And just as important, he shows us how to use them. Each time we ask God for help in our struggles and concerns, we open the tool chest of our hearts and ask him to give us **what** we need, **when** we need it, according to his will. And he will always answer us.

Our perception of truth is colored by our quest for knowledge, information and ideas... for what we can learn about the world around us. I believe that when our search is conducted honestly and earnestly, we reach the ultimate discovery that

✢ How do I Grow in knowledge and wisdom?

the only truth we can count on is what flows from the heart of God and the life of Jesus Christ.

What we know influences how we think, and how we think affects how we feel. Thoughts travel quickly from the head to the heart. The old saying, "Garbage in, garbage out," is more true today than ever before (and there's a lot of garbage out there!). What we soak up as "human sponges" can either be life-giving water or undiluted poison... or more commonly, water laced with poison. We've got to be careful about the knowledge we absorb.

By allowing knowledge to expand our awareness of the world, we add real depth to our lives. It's like viewing life in 3-D instead of 2-D vision, as our love of knowledge brings about a love for the created world in which we live out God's story. And an appreciation and love of God's almighty power which he demonstrated in creating our unique role in the reality he fashioned for us.

We can change the way we think about knowledge. It will certainly teach us about people, places and events, and we can also look at these things from an eternal perspective... from God's point of view.

How do you acquire your knowledge? Do you **passively** receive it or **actively** seek it? Ask yourself, "Does knowledge have value for me or does it just take up space on my bookshelf?"

When it comes to feeding and nourishing the empty spaces in your brain with the wondrous events of history, the issues that affect contemporary life and the wisdom that emerges from our search for truth, it is surely better to actively seek knowledge than to passively receive it through the world's corrupted channels. All too often, we are inclined to receive passive entertainment from media events, athletic contests or non-productive activities. But we can actively learn so much more about the world through other sources of knowledge and information.

What can actively-sought knowledge do that passively-acquired knowledge can't? Well, it can heighten our perceptions about life in general, from both a practical and philosophical standpoint. And it leads to personal insight. We learn about God and how world events conform or conflict with his love and mercy, his creation and redemption. We are led by the Holy Spirit to an eternal perspective with our sights set on Christ and our heavenly Father's kingdom.

Another practical by-product of our quest for knowledge is the desire to teach others what we know, sharing what we've learned from our life experience, the information we've received and the wisdom we've gained. In a wonderful way, this process allows the teacher to become the student. After all, much of the educational process involves providing information, insight and ideas while listening to ourselves in the process.

> Ever-expanding knowledge about the world around us creates fertile ground for the gift of wisdom.

When you do share your knowledge, you allow your mind to open more broadly to the possibility of even further insights about what you already know.

Ever-expanding knowledge about the world around us creates fertile ground for the gift of wisdom. We actually receive wisdom as a gift of the Holy Spirit which helps us see life from God's point of view, from an eternal perspective. What a payoff! Just think about that – as you see your world, community, family and personal events from a divine perspective, you create a seedbed for the growth of God's wisdom within you!

■ NEVER THOUGHT YOU'D NEED LATIN?

Educare is the Latin term from which we derive the English word "educate" and it means "to guide" or "to lead." It does **not** mean "to teach," although most educators would consider themselves teachers. *Educare* connotes the idea of leading from one thing to another… from ignorance to knowledge… from darkness to light! Readjust your concept of education based on its Latin root meaning. You will then see yourself in a new way – as one who actively guides, leads, mentors, advises, counsels… in short, someone who can touch the hearts, minds and souls of others.

Look for someone younger than you who might benefit from your friendship, influence and guidance. Become their mentor. Invite that person to share a cup of coffee or lunch with you from time to time. Talk about their interests. Listen well. Offer advice when asked. And if you don't know, just say so. That is also an opportunity for you to stretch and learn more.

In a similar way, if you have a family, pray that your own children will cross paths with adults who can be a positive influence on them. As parents, we cannot meet all our children's needs and expectations, and outside help can certainly reduce the void that remains. That's one of the reasons my own four sons have been involved in Scouting. It's not just about outdoor skills and merit badges – it's also about the adult role models they have encountered.

One of the best ways we can communicate our knowledge is by personally sharing stories, situations and struggles in our own lives. I love telling family stories to my kids and they love hearing them. They learn real-world lessons about dealing with dilemmas, difficulties, even disasters, while becoming more firmly connected to their ancestral heritage.

■ DOES YOUR MIND NEED EXERCISE?

Make learning a lifetime process. Seek new information and knowledge every day. Your brain can handle it! Like a muscle, your mind needs regular exercise to stay fit. Look for creative ways to gather knowledge beyond the traditional approaches that use printed material and media.

For example, talk to others about their work, their roles as parent, friend and employee. As discussed in the "Relationships" **LifeWork Area,** talk to the elderly about the wisdom they have gained. They have much to share – if we will just take the time to listen and learn.

Gather family history from older relatives that can tell you about your ancestors. What were they like? Collect photographs and attach memories to them.

My friend Jim is an avid family historian, tracing his roots back to the Civil War era. His great grandfather served in a New York artillery battalion. Jim learned of a New Yorker who was writing about this Civil War group of soldiers, and he began to correspond with the author. He received copies of letters written by various members who refer by name to his great grandfather. He was thrilled!

And the thrill escalated when Jim learned that an Internet auction was taking place for various Civil War photographs recently discovered after being in storage for decades. Some of the photos featured the New York Artillery Battalion. He got on his computer just in time to find that all but one picture remained... his great grandfather! He won the photo with a winning bid of $100.

As Jim shared this story with me, he asked if I'd like to see the picture. "Sure," I said and there he was – a handsome young man in a Union Army uniform. On the back side of the photo was his great grandfather's signature. What a treasure!

■ CAN YOU KNOW GOD INTELLECTUALLY?

Our intellect was created by God. When we nourish it with knowledge, we expand our capacity for **confident** existence in the world around us.

The more we know about the world, the more we know about the God who created it. Life is about knowing, loving and serving the God who made us. Guided by the Holy Spirit, we follow Christ in doing the Father's will (in his story). This is what prepares us for experiencing true joy in this world and the next.

And the more we come to know God, the more we will trust him in all things. It is very much a father-child relationship. In a loving home, the child knows he can trust Dad to protect, guide, teach and support him.

But how do we "know" the unseen God? Through faith and experience. We "experience" God especially through his Word. Through prayer and worship. Through the voice of the Holy Spirit dwelling within us. Through the blessings of people we know and love. Through strangers we meet. Through the miracle of life. And through the example of men and women through the ages who lived their lives for him in complete trust and self-surrender.

Even though God is mystery, he has revealed himself and his eternal plan to us in his Son, Jesus Christ. He has left us plenty of signs that he is real: Start with the created world and the larger universe. Think about the incredible complexity of all that surrounds us, from swirling galaxies to single-cell life forms, and ponder the divine architect who designed these systems to operate so perfectly and intelligently. I can practically guarantee that as your knowledge of the world increases, so will your faith in the one who created it.

■ HOW IS THE BIBLE LIKE THE "BREATH OF GOD?"

God's Word, communicated to us especially in the Bible, provides us with the most reliable source of truth in the world. In the Armenian culture from which I come, the word for the Bible means "Breath of God." And in the original Hebrew, the word for the Holy Spirit means "Breath of God." Interesting! As the Holy Spirit breathes the truth of the Word into our lives, his truth deeply touches our hearts and souls as well – so that we can live the truth. And, in turn, Christ can touch others through us.

As we make discoveries about God, we can record them in a journal (see page 147 for more information on *The LifeWork Principle Journal*), talk about them with others, and, **most importantly**, live them. It all starts with prayer and reading the Bible, the written Word of God.

We are on an earthly journey to the Father. The choices we make, the steps we take, will either lead us to him or away from him. It's like a freeway that leads us to our ultimate destination, yet which is intersected with avenues of trials, temptations and sin that can take us off course and lead to spiritual dead ends. Christ and his church provide sturdy guardrails along that freeway, but our own free will can lead us to take wrong turns. Fortunately, God allows u-turns, and he can forgive and restore us on our journey.

■ How can the mind enhance the heart?

Are you truly passionate about something in your life? Instead of letting knowledge quench that passion; rather, we can use knowledge as a means to deepen that passion.

Why is this important? Because the one, single passion that rises above all other passions, interests and pursuits has a spiritual dimension; that is the passion for God and his Son, Jesus Christ – and the gift of faith God freely offers to us. It is a passion for truth.

Deepening your passion for God may result in blessings like:

- The light of Christ illuminating your life with untold grace.

- The passion you have for pursuits in this world taking on new meaning.

- The will of the Father becoming more obvious with each passing day.

■ What kind of pipeline are you connected to?

Supplements to Scripture include devotional books, spiritual audio and video resources, conferences and retreats. And look for the daily miracles all around us in nature, technology and human interaction. Beyond these things is the normal flow of knowledge – from classrooms, newspapers, magazines, books, television and movies. Just be <u>careful</u> about what you consume, especially if it comes through the world's pipeline.

Consider television, movies, videogames or the Internet: while they can be a pipeline for truth, beauty and helpful knowledge, they are more often collection centers for the sewage of immorality that's dumped on us daily. Let's take an honest, critical look at what we allow to come into our homes and hearts. And just as we deal with clutter on a desk, we can be aggressively ruthless in getting rid of the unnecessary, the unacceptable, the objectionable.

What kinds of pipelines are connected to your home, clean or dirty? How do they influence **your soul** and the **souls of your children**? It's time to disconnect and cap off the pipelines that transport the sewage of our corrupt culture. Replace those pipes with the fresh springs of God's goodness – and enjoy life-giving grace now and for eternity.

Chapter 5

SOCIETY

I once owned a Toyota Land Cruiser – 5,300 pounds of heavyweight SUV transportation. (Frankly, at that weight, there wasn't much "sport" in this sport utility vehicle!) On my frequent business trips, I would securely ensconce myself in the Land Cruiser's bank-vault enclosure of steel, and bully my way up and down the freeways of central California, impervious to the dangers around me. Nothing could harm me; nothing could stop me.

Then one afternoon as I began a three-hour trip home from a meeting, I heard a loud "thud" at 65 miles per hour. Within 20 seconds, I was at a standstill with no air in my left rear tire, the victim of foreign-object intrusion on the freeway. I was stranded on a narrow embankment of dirt, just off the highway. I was no longer invincible. My Land Cruiser was paralyzed, powerless to protect me.

I got roadside assistance from an emergency worker and eventually resumed my trip home. Without his help, I would not have been able to get back on the freeway.

What a powerful reminder of how important it is to help others in need… those who are broken down, stranded or in need of repair – whether physical, emotional, mental or spiritual. This episode also illustrates how we can rely on the help of others in our own lives. We are all in this life together, and we are all called by the Father to be transformed into the image and likeness of God to those we encounter daily… to reflect the light of Christ to them.

Allow God to challenge your comfortable life. Ask him what you can do to fill the needs of others. Why? Because that's the example Jesus gave us. It is abundantly clear in the Bible that Jesus was particularly concerned about the poor, the sick and the needy – and if that's his concern, and if we truly belong to him, it is our concern as well.

As obedient sons and daughters of God, we can make a personal commitment to pursue the countless ways we can help others. As the Bible teaches us: "You shall love your neighbor as yourself" (Matthew 22:39).

We normally see our local community as a source of comfort and acceptance, but we can also view it as a source of need; seeing the world not only for what it offers **to us,** but for what **we** can offer in return. By this healthy balance, we can help satisfy the needs of others according to God's will. The light of Christ is reflected through us to those who need the brilliance of God's love – even for those who don't realize how much he is needed in their lives. In this way, the Holy Spirit directs us so that we become a lighthouse, shining it's beacon to give direction to others.

> Help the poor –
> whether their hunger
> is for food or faith.

It all comes down to this question: will you live a self-centered life or a life that extends its branches, shade and fruitfulness to those in the world around you? To live the latter means going **beyond** your immediate frame of reference and familiar relationships, **beyond** your immediate family and friends, **beyond** your comfort zone. It may take you to new frontiers and unfamiliar places. Yet Christ lives there too! He lives in the hearts, minds and souls of the poor just as he does in those who live in comfort. His love extends beyond church walls and flows into taverns, prisons and homeless shelters. As part of our mission, we are sent by God into some of these settings to help the lowly and less fortunate; to engage them with the same compassion that Jesus showed to so many.

Help the poor – whether their hunger is for food or faith. Within the next 60 seconds, can you think of at least **one** person or **one** local church or world organization that you can assist in some way to reach the poor, the sick and the needy? They can be part of your mission in life.

❧ HOW CAN I LIVE AN ACTIVE FAITH?

Think beyond those in material poverty, and include those who may be in mental, spiritual or emotional poverty. Tap into **your** talents and gifts. Seek ways to help them. The blessings that accompany service to others will flow to them **through you**. Thus the light of Christ will be reflected in your life and actions.

The rewards of helping others are truly gifts from God – they become part of the ongoing process of bearing fruit. He finds ways to bless those that extend the hand of help to others. You **will** experience great satisfaction in living an **active** faith, allowing Jesus to use you as a vessel, pouring out his love, mercy and goodness over the world.

■ HOW CAN SOMEONE BE BOTH RICH AND POOR?

While much of our focus is typically placed on relieving material poverty, we cannot overlook spiritual poverty. Nor can we overlook the materially wealthy and realize that they also have needs. Do you know someone in a middle- or upper-class position that is spiritually poor? Pray about it, maybe this is someone Christ wants to help through you.

And if you have been blessed with material well-being, think how you can share your money and possessions with others. I have a friend who gives away one or two items of clothing for every item he purchases. If he buys a shirt, he gives away two shirts. He's not rich by any means, but he knows how to share the blessings of material comfort with others while cutting back on clutter – a real win-win situation for everyone!

We often forget about the needs of the world beyond our own country – from those living in abject poverty to victims of natural disasters, from the persecuted to the marginalized. As mentioned earlier, Jesus had a special concern for the poor, the sick and the needy. We can adopt his attitude, and become authentically concerned with sharing, giving and helping others in need.

We are challenged to a dual perspective on richness. If we are financially secure and our needs for money and material acquisitions have been met, how can we share our wealth with others? And, no matter what our economic circumstances, how can we address the needs of the wealthy, particularly in spiritual ways?

I'll never forget an image I witnessed as a college student at the University of California at Berkeley. Near the campus was a facility that helped the disabled gain independence for living on their own, and it was common to see people from the facility on or near the campus. As I walked to class one morning from my apartment, I saw two young men coming toward me, one in a wheelchair and the other pushing him. As we passed each other, I noticed that the fellow in the wheelchair was a quadriplegic, paralyzed from the neck down. The man pushing him was blind. What a powerful picture of how we can help one another, regardless of our own limitations!

■ WHERE ARE YOU COMING FROM?

To keep it all in perspective, view heaven as our true, eternal home and earth as our temporary home in exile. We live a temporary existence here, but all that we do on earth has eternal consequences. The soul we touch today will affect other souls now and in future generations.

Pursue those things that will not pass away, that will remain when you are gone – like sharing the faith, spreading God's love and modeling virtues like humility and hope.

What we do today creates ripples in the lake of time and eternity... a lake without a shoreline. In other words, even the smallest action we take produces consequences - for better or worse - for future generations into all eternity. Which will it be? It's up to us. When we extend the hand of kindness or embody the virtue of humility, we are sure to affect others in ways that only God knows. It is the practice of these types of virtues that keep the ripples moving ever-outward, impacting one soul after another.

■ WHO'S YOUR DOCTOR?

As a vocational rehabilitation consultant, I encountered four situations over a 12-month period involving people who had lost both legs – three adult men and one young boy, all seriously injured in accidents, and a relatively rare situation in my practice. What struck me most about these people was their attitude. In today's culture of victimhood, it would be easy for these people to be filled with bitterness about their impairments. But to me, their responses were nothing short of heroic! Each of them overcame any feelings of despair and "rose to the occasion," becoming engaged in activities that emphasized their abilities rather than their disabilities.

> In a spiritual sense, we are all injured, broken, wounded, impaired and disabled.

Over the years, I've seen a wide range of injuries and trauma resulting in permanent disabilities; people that are broken and in need of repair. Often times, medical treatment can only go so far, and may not always bring someone back to a 100% functional level. It then becomes a matter of adapting and accepting the limitations, moving on with life.

But in a spiritual sense, we are all injured, broken, wounded, impaired and disabled. We are in need of restoration, and Jesus is our divine physician. He takes what we can do and helps us do it better. He takes our wounds and heals us of them. He takes our scars and removes them from us. He makes us whole again. This is his love in action.

Go to him in prayer. Lay your problems before him. Then let him step in, take over and restore you to health!

■ WHO ARE YOUR HEROES?

It's been said that America's greatest generation was that of the World War II era. Why? Because that generation produced **true heroes** that fill our minds and hearts with inspiring stories of courage and bravery in the face of great peril, even death. These were men and women of strong character who embodied the ideals of self-sacrifice for the greater good. They were also great citizens and patriots, many contributing significantly after the war to their communities. But the time for heroes is not past: in our generation, in our own situation in life, we too are called to be heroes for today.

Look for heroes. Look in both the past and present. And expand your definition of what makes a "hero." Heroes don't necessarily have to be "larger than life," but can even be people you know that embody the qualities of courage, resilience and sacrifice. In fact, they are everywhere: cops on violent streets, military in hazardous situations overseas, firefighters going into burning buildings, teachers in schools, parents taking care of their families.

For example, if one of your friends has a servant's heart and you admire the impressive way this is lived out, consider that person a hero – a role model. Think of him or her often, and ask yourself how they would respond to the challenging situations in which you find yourself.

Of course, our greatest role model is Jesus Christ. In him, we find the best example of how to live a life worth living. The popular phrase "what would Jesus do?" is a good question, and one that challenges us to move beyond the question into action.

Having role models is a sure-fire way to adopt personal qualities that are important to you. I'm occasionally called upon to speak publicly, either to a large group or in broadcast interviews. I look to certain role models whose poise, confidence and speaking style I admire, and this has helped me improve my ability to communicate effectively. I'm still learning, but I have some good instructors!

■ DOES GOD CARE ABOUT OUR SACRIFICES?

Ah, the big one: sacrifice. Something we're not used to. The warning label attached to the word "sacrifice" says "Caution: may require stepping out of your comfort zone."

Sacrifice: learn it, live it, love it. Jesus did – his was the ultimate sacrifice on the cross, offered for our sins and for our salvation. The motion picture *The Passion of the Christ* pulls no punches about Jesus' sacrifice, and we see there graphically what he willingly endured for us. Anything we might do pales in comparison, yet our sacrifices mean a great deal to the God who made us:

Sacrifice means:

- GIVING your time to help others.

- SHARING your possessions and material wealth.

- PROVIDING for the needs of the poor and disadvantaged.

- DOING the right thing, not the comfortable thing.

- BEING faithful, not successful.

- HELPING others get to heaven by introducing them to God.

- STEPPING outside your ego and pride in acts of humility, kindness and charity.

■ IS IT DANGEROUS TO "DO IT ALL?"

We can get so caught up in our little world of Saturday barbecues, kids' sporting events and the latest movie, that we develop a type of tunnel vision. Left unchecked, our "busyness" can gain momentum and literally send our lives out of control.

It's important that we protect our free time, because it is then that we refresh ourselves on all levels – physically, mentally, emotionally and spiritually. The old Armenian proverb, "You can't hold two watermelons in one hand," frequently comes to mind when my life demands more balance.

We can achieve balance if we are open to the guidance of the Holy Spirit and choose those activities and responsibilities that are most important before God; to fulfilling the Father's will.

We can't "do it all" – and when we try, we often become limited in our effectiveness, efficiency and enjoyment of the activity.

Chapter 6

FITNESS

My friend Bob had just installed a new transmission in his '63 Chevy, converting it from its original "3-on-the-tree" column shift to the infinitely cooler "4-on-the-floor" design.

One Friday night, he was showing his girlfriend how quickly he could shift while racing down the city's main drag. Attempting a "power shift" (applying full throttle while quickly tapping the clutch between shifts), a gear was missed and an ugly, grinding sound shrieked out of his transmission case. He had virtually destroyed his new 4-speed gearbox with the exception of one gear: reverse.

Bob spent the next 2 hours driving backwards across town to get his girlfriend home, taking side streets and trying to see the road by the dim illumination of his backup lights.

That's the night Bob discovered that his car had limitations, and that he had exceeded them. He was forced to choose an alternative method of travel – ironically, not only being forced to drive in reverse, but also with limited light, making it all the more difficult to see the road.

Like Bob's Chevy, we were designed to operate properly within a certain set of limitations. To operate at optimum efficiency without exceeding those limitations, our focus is on how to achieve and then maintain health of body, mind and spirit. Poor fitness can prevent us from seeing the road ahead, and makes us only dimly aware of our progress. Ultimately, it can keep us from moving forward toward our eternal destination. Staying on course depends largely on staying fit and balanced in the **7 LifeWork Areas**.

Fitness doesn't apply only to your physical body. Yes, your body is out of shape when there is too little or too much weight, poor muscle tone or an unhealthy diet. But your **mind** can also be out of shape when it absorbs too little or too much information, or the wrong kind of information. And **your spirit** can be out of shape when you give in to temptation and sin, or when spiritual dehydration occurs due to a lack of the kind of food and drink that comes from living the spiritual life. Seek fitness in **every** dimension of your life.

A healthy lifestyle for the body, mind and spirit (and a healthy **balance** between them) provides a rock-solid foundation for getting through life in good shape.

We often forget how closely integrated body, mind and spirit really are. When the body feels pain, we have a mental reaction to it. When our mind is challenged by an unfortunate turn in events, we sense the effect on our spirit. And when we are spiritually hungry, our control of the body and mind is weakened.

Like everything else around us, the dimensions of body, mind and spirit are unique gifts from God who created us. Just as the Father has mapped out a highly unique and personal plan for each of us, he has also given us the special combination of body, mind and spirit to provide the means for being who he wants us to be and doing what he wants us to do. But we have to cultivate the gift.

It's a decision between actively seeking a healthy lifestyle or staying just the way you are. Even if you are reasonably fit right now, there is a maintenance aspect of fitness that we cannot overlook. A fit lifestyle is just that: a lifestyle that seeks health and fitness on a regular basis in the areas of body, mind and spirit.

Failure to pursue a fit lifestyle leads to bad habits and a decline in personal health. Think how easy it is to gain five pounds a year! (Or more!) What kind of person do you truly want to be? Fit or flabby?

To ensure **physical fitness:** Good diet and regular exercise. Simple.

To ensure **mental fitness:** Entertain good, positive thoughts, emotions and reactions to events, people and circumstances with an eternal perspective, dispelling negative, invasive thoughts like anger, impurity, worry. Read informative, good books. Stop gossip, sarcasm, put-downs, name-calling and criticism of others.

To ensure **spiritual fitness**: Pray and read Scripture daily. Be aware of the presence of the Holy Spirit in your life. Join in regular community worship. Trust and hope in Christ.

The payoff? Increased energy across the board – a stronger body, mind and spirit. A vibrant ability to penetrate the haze of the world around you, and see God more clearly in all things. What can be better than that?

■ WHAT'S THE SETTING OF YOUR "EMOTIONAL THERMOSTAT?"

Our emotions are closely related to what is going on in our mind, body and spirit. By having a strong spiritual foundation and confidence that God is in control, we can diminish unhealthy reactions and overreactions.

So what's the setting of your emotional thermostat? If it's set **too high**, you may find yourself out-of-control, angry, sullen or sarcastic – all of which subtracts from the light of Christ we are asked to reflect in a dark world. **Too low**, and you may run the risk of being emotionally distant, cold and unapproachable… again, far from the type of person God intends you to be.

To keep your emotional thermostat in balance, think of the word "halt" as an acronym, which can remind you to adjust your thermostat when you are **Hungry, Angry, Lonely** or **Tired**. These feelings frequently trigger inappropriate actions and reactions, so it pays to recognize circumstances in which you run the risk of "overheating" or "running cold," and to make adjustments to your emotional thermostat to prevent that from occurring.

Steve, my workout partner at the gym, told me the saga of the hard-boiled eggs he prepares in bulk each week as a source of protein. He normally takes two out of the refrigerator daily, carefully warming them in the microwave oven for 15 seconds or so to take the chill off, then pops them into his mouth one at a time. His routine worked perfectly until recently, when he bit into an egg that had retained a hidden concentration of heat. The egg exploded, plastering its contents all over his face, floor and furniture! Steve didn't realize how much heat had built up until the explosion occurred. And, on an emotional level, sometimes neither do we. So we need to set our emotional thermostat to keep our emotions in balance. And when our emotions are in balance, we experience peace.

■ "JUST DO IT" – DOES IT REALLY WORK?

Healthy food, regular exercise and an active lifestyle have so many bonuses it would be futile to attempt to cover them all here. Just go for it… do it… and if you don't have a healthy diet, get one. You know what to do and if you don't, there is **plenty** of advice on the bookshelves. If you don't know how – or how much – to exercise, get advice from your doctor, go to a personal trainer or read books on the subject.

If you're new to exercise, start **gradually**. When I first began jogging years ago, I couldn't even make a city block. Adding distance, block by block, helped me get to the point where I could run 10K races on a regular basis. Years later, the same principle of gradual progression applied to lifting weights, with slow but steady increases in the amount of weight and the number of repetitions.

Getting started in the first place is a victory in itself! The most important step in walking, jogging, cycling or going to the gym is the step you take out your front door. Anyone who walks into our local health club, no matter what their shape, size or age, gets my respect. Why? Because they came! They recognized that change wouldn't occur until they made the first move.

REGULAR EXERCISE COUPLED WITH PROPER NUTRITION AND REST CAN ALLOW FOR:

- Weight loss
- Improved cardiovascular function
- Stress relief
- Improved muscle tone, definition or size
- Feeling better (because we're healthier!)

■ HOW'S YOUR SPIRITUAL FITNESS?

Our spiritual life requires regular nourishment and exercise. We go to the fountain of grace through the "exercise" of regular prayer, study and worship to nourish who we are as sons and daughters of God, as followers of Christ. If we don't, we'll find ourselves parched and spiritually dry.

> Our spiritual life requires regular nourishment and exercise.

One of the big events in the life of a Cub Scout is the annual Space Derby, in which propeller-driven "spaceships" race one another along parallel strings stretched high across the room. Having four sons, I've helped each of them construct a wide variety of cosmic cruisers over the years.

One particular spaceship really stands out. My son and I spent a great deal of time carefully shaping the styrofoam body with the ultimate in precision designer tools: a potato peeler. Unfortunately, we should have taken more time choosing the paint for our spacecraft. We simply grabbed a convenient can of spray lacquer, took aim and fired away with a blast of paint... that immediately melted the styrofoam into a crispy, shapeless blob. We went from "Star Trek" to "star wreck" at warp speed!

But we learned a lesson about the relationship between the fragile body of a styrofoam spaceship and the destructive power of lacquer paint. It's a lot like our relationship with sin, in which the image of Christ in our souls becomes distorted and corrupted when sin touches us with its toxicity. But unlike styrofoam, we can repent and be re-formed through the mercy, forgiveness and grace of God. And then – we start over!

I've seen lives broken down by evil and sin – and witnessed the intervention of Jesus so that the brokenness can be repaired and restored.

But don't underestimate Satan's commitment to destroy those who believe in God. He will tempt us with the false attractions of glossy magazines, movies and media, with the so-called "adult" content found on the Internet and cable channels, and with the promise of pleasure from possessions, power and personal achievement.

Ignatius of Loyola, a respected 16th century spiritual writer, said that there are three voices within us: the voice of **Satan** who longs to destroy us, to make certain we are self-centered and prideful; the voice of **self**, manifested by our thoughts, words, emotions and actions; and finally, the voice of **God** who loves us completely, 100% of the time, and wants us to attain eternal life through Jesus Christ in heaven.

Which voice do we listen to? It's probably a **mixture** of all three. When we hear the voice of **evil**, we can immediately invoke the protection of Jesus. He will rebuke Satan and surround us with his cloak of goodness and grace.

To avoid sin, we can choose to avoid the **situations** that can lead to sin. It is not in our power to avoid all temptation – after all, we know from the Bible that even Jesus was tempted – but we can stay away from **unnecessary** temptation.

If we're trapped in habitual sin, even enslaved by it, then we still have the choice of stopping – to just say "no." To say "enough of this." This may require continual turning back to God, asking for his mercy, forgiveness and grace, and making commitments to change our lives to follow Christ more closely.

I realize this is much easier said than done, but Christ can free us from the bonds of evil, and by the grace of God, we can change. With some types of habitual sin, particularly negative addictions, deep healing is often necessary. Jesus is our divine physician, and many churches offer recovery ministries that have helped millions cope with hurts, habits and hang-ups.

Let the Holy Spirit guide you in recognizing the presence of sin and bad habits – then take those burdens to Jesus for forgiveness and healing.

■ WHAT CAN YOU LEARN FROM A JOCK?

The athlete develops self-discipline in order to perform well. Peak performance requires intensive training, daily practice, proper nutrition and mental focus. We can learn from this. If self-discipline pays off on the playing field, it will also pay off in real life.

It's all about self-mastery – gaining control over our desires for pleasure, possessions, power and prestige, and directing them to God. This takes serious effort on a daily – sometimes hourly – basis.

Why is self-mastery so difficult? In a word: **pride**. Pride gives us a false sense of power and control, and keeps us from pursuing many of the ideas discussed in this book: surrender, sacrifice, humility, patience and a host of other key virtues. It also keeps us from being peacemakers in disputes with others. When **it** comes to pride, control it or it will control **you**! For that, we need God's grace.

And while there are valuable lessons in the athletic discipline found in many sports, it's good to also put athletics into an eternal perspective. Why do we get so wildly enthusiastic about watching a ball fly through the air? Whether it is thrown through a hoop, batted into a glove, kicked through a goalpost or putted into a hole, the bottom line is: it's only a ball.

Don't get me wrong – I love watching competitive sports. But if only we could capture even a fraction of the enthusiasm we have for that ball and redirect that excitement to God! He truly deserves our enthusiasm – after all, he created all things, including us! What an amazing, profound, incredible blessing our Father has given us – to be his sons and daughters with his gift of eternal life.

■ Do healthy kids become healthy adults?

Getting kids involved with good food and regular exercise will plant the seeds of fitness that will continue growing long after they stop being young. Children's sports are a good introduction to a fit lifestyle, and help them learn the importance of a healthy balance between protein, fat and carbohydrates, and the value of cardio/aerobic exercise and muscle tone.

This is one of the most practical and beneficial things we can offer our kids in today's fast-food-obsessed, sugar-saturated, carb-crazy society that seems to be getting more out of shape with each passing year. There is real power in controlling **what** we eat, **when** we eat and **how** we view food. It is one aspect of personal self-discipline and self-mastery.

As for myself, I admit it! – I'm a recovering "chip-aholic." I loved relaxing with a bag of salty, crispy chips, and often found myself mindlessly munching them at various times throughout each day. Chips were my comfort food, and I justified my addiction by telling myself I was "entitled" to enjoy chips as a "reward" for all my hard work. So after a grueling day of discussions, depositions and defending my opinions, I would pick up a bag of my favorite ranch-flavored tortilla chips and munch all the way home.

We can do all kinds of mental gymnastics with ourselves and even our kids, justifying junk food – and even fast food – because "they like it" or "there's no time to cook" or "at least it's chicken." Of course, there's a time and place for fun, convenient foods. But if left unchecked, then it is easy to let good tastes become a bad habit. And our weight become overweight!

■ WHY DEVELOP AN "ATTITUDE OF GRATITUDE?"

Let us never forget to give thanks to God in all things. When I was an infant, my father came down with what was then a life-threatening disease: **coccidioidomycosis**, or "Valley Fever." He nearly died, but by the grace of God and extensive medical treatment, he survived. In thanks to God, my father lived a devout spiritual life for the remainder of his years. I always remember that example of gratitude.

In fact, I believe an "attitude of gratitude" is part of a fit lifestyle; to be thankful for the many blessings we receive in body, mind and spirit. Failing to do that with God and others assumes that it's all automatic – that good health is simply the result of being "lucky."

Take a close look at your life, and do an inventory of things you are thankful for: Do you have a good job? Educational opportunities? A loving spouse? Children? Good parents? A good friend? Health?

Express your gratitude in prayer, word and action. The more you do this, the more you'll come to know God. The more you know God, the more you will trust him. The more you trust him, the more you will hope in him and surrender your life to him and his will.

Chapter 7

LEISURE

I have held an interest in old cars since my youth. I began by drawing cars, then building models of them, progressing to restoring them, showing them and collecting a wide range of automobilia. Unfortunately, what started as a hobby later evolved into a grand obsession. Each day started and ended with a craving for more cars, more hard-to-find parts and more rare automobile literature. I bought and sold many classic vehicles, telling myself that each purchase would be a "keeper," only to eventually lose interest and replace that vehicle with another *car du jour.*

In short, I found that I was using my leisure time to succumb to the gravity of worldly possessions. It was all about accumulating material "things" rather than enjoying a rest and retreat from them. Yet leisure is time to be "receptive" rather than "productive."

A hobby can turn leisure time into a healthy, fulfilling thing – a time for renewal and relaxation in body, mind and spirit. Or it can spin wildly out of control and dominate our leisure time with unhealthy obsessions and ambitions. How do you spend your leisure time?

Our pursuit of leisure is so strong that it often becomes our sole reward for hard work, for a job well done. We work, save and plan for all kinds of leisure activities, and spend much of our lives just thinking about them. Even the mere **anticipation** of leisure becomes a source of happiness! Well-channeled leisure affects us in all the other **LifeWork Areas.** In fact, we can successfully integrate leisure with faith, family, friends, fitness and even work. That's the challenge: to balance our lives in the **7 LifeWork Areas.**

⚜ WHY IS LEISURE TIME NECESSARY?

Like rest after exercise, leisure time allows for **rest, relaxation** and **recovery** of our skills so we can use them again and again. We are refreshed, restored, renewed, and often find that leisure redirects our skills in new and exciting ways.

Here's how to reset our view of leisure in two ways: **First,** see leisure as necessary, not just a place to park the leftovers of available time. **Second,** use leisure in ways that enhance our talents, rather than in ways that misuse or waste them.

In our leisure time, we make decisions whether to seek activities that lead us to the good, the pure, the self-giving and the enriching – or to seek activities that lead us to temptation, sin, self-centeredness and self-indulgence. The menu of choices served up by the world typically involves more bad than good and our choices are often between the wholesome or garbage. There is barely any "gray area" or middle ground here.

In matters of leisure, just ask yourself: Is this the best use of my time? Is this going to lead me in a good direction, or into a state of separation from God? Often, it's the answers to these questions that determine whether the use of leisure time is good or bad. Seek the guidance of the Holy Spirit as you choose those activities that will enrich all your other **LifeWork Areas.**

There is a direct and proportionate relationship between the quality of our leisure time and all the other **LifeWork Areas.** As we improve, increase and expand the leisure in our life, we find that the world around us gets bigger and brighter. As leisure is integrated into our LifeWork, it helps us to be receptive and listen to the voice of God, and so use time more wisely. Leisure becomes an important and necessary element in our road trip of life.

■ IS LAUGHTER REALLY THE BEST MEDICINE?

Let me encourage you to participate in the relentless pursuit of… humor. Yes, humor! There are times when I think the best possible use of our leisure time is spent **laughing**. Sharing funny stories, watching a classic comedy, listening to a clean stand-up comic.

The more we engage in good humor, the more likely we are to develop a positive disposition of cheerfulness – being more upbeat, optimistic and prone to smiling.

One of my sons is **not** a "natural smiler." When he was 14, I began encouraging him to make an effort to smile more, letting him know that a good first impression for a young man to make is simply to smile. Six months later, he came up to me at a church dinner function to tell me that "this smiling stuff really works!" He and his fellow Boy Scouts had been in charge of busing the tables, and quite unexpectedly, he found that his smile was earning him tips!

So learn to laugh heartily, smile frequently and share your cheerful nature generously with those around you. They'll be happier and so will you!

■ ENTERTAINMENT OR ENTRAPMENT?

The entertainment world is overflowing with good and bad choices, more bad than good. We have to be **very careful** in choosing the movies and television we watch, the printed material we read and the events we attend. We need to be especially careful if we have children; they are so impressionable and easily influenced.

If our eyes are the windows to our soul, then we can use our eyes as **filters**, as ways to **screen out** garbage and junk. Custody of the heart begins with custody of the eyes.

We can ask ourselves questions such as: what does entertainment mean before God? How do I define and distinguish positive, good entertainment from negative, bad entertainment? How can I improve the ways in which I experience entertainment?

It's good to honestly look at our answers, because they can show us when we are predisposed to good versus bad, to pure versus impure, to wholesome versus corrupted. We are forced to look at our **character**. The kind of person we are is defined by the **choices** we make, including our entertainment choices. I love what former U.S. Congressman J. C. Watts said: "Character is doing what's right when nobody's looking."

■ CAN A HARMLESS HOBBY GO TOO FAR?

Our hobbies can become so large a part of our lives that we become almost one-dimensional. We **become** our hobby: We **are** golf. We **are** a classic car. We **are** a quilt. There is one key word to keep at the forefront of our hobbies: **balance**. Keep things in check. **Watch out** if your hobby begins to spin out of control in the areas of time, money and thoughts.

If that occurs, then your hobby can swiftly move to a new category: a negative obsession. Your waking moments are filled with thoughts related to your passion for sports or shopping or cars or collectibles. To the exclusion of other and better thoughts.

Back when my hobby was restoring pre-war Fords, I learned at club meets and car shows that there is only one language to be spoken: Ford. Intense discussions and debates were common about such minutia as the proper location of a "Danger: Hot" warning tag as it was originally affixed to new 1936 Fords rolling out of the factory. Was it placed on the top of the radiator hose, on the radiator itself, or perhaps on the clamp that went around the radiator hose?

You get the idea. Get too deeply into your hobby, and you'll be distracted from the things that really matter – things with eternal implications.

■ WHERE TO?

One of the best things you can do with your free time is "go somewhere." See more of the world around you. Experience other cultures – the food, the language, the people, the scenery, the history. This does much to increase your worldview of God's creation and illuminate the needs of others less fortunate than us. Even a one-hour drive will have a positive effect. The benefits become multiplied by going even further to unfamiliar areas.

> Use a portion of your leisure time doing nothing, just resting.

Travel allows us to detach from our familiar, day-to-day world and refresh our body, mind and spirit with new sights and experiences. Think of a place you can go in the next 30 days, even if it's just a day trip or weekend getaway. Plan it, and then do it! And while you're away, plan an even bigger trip you can take within the next 12 months.

■ DOES DOING NOTHING DO ANYTHING?

It's tempting to schedule our leisure time so that it is no longer "leisure" time, but "scheduled" time. That's when leisure time begins to feel like work. Use a portion of your leisure time doing nothing, just resting. No activities, no TV, no hobbies. Take a nap. Sit on the front porch. Recline and listen to music. It is in these times, when we are receptive, that God often speaks to our heart. Our body, mind and spirit have the opportunity to be refreshed, renewed and restored.

Once a friend asked me if I ever just sat and did nothing. I said yes, explaining that I often just sit and play my guitar, read a magazine or have coffee with a friend. He corrected me and said, "That's doing **something** – I mean doing **nothing**."

He made a good point. And since considering my friend's question, I've actually done it – just sat myself down on the front porch and done… **nothing**. And you know what? It was nice. I had time to think, to pray and simply let my mind go blank. I was unplugged from the hectic pace of daily activity and I discovered a new way of being refreshed. And now I owe my friend a cup of coffee!

■ WHAT PART OF "YOU CAN'T TAKE IT WITH YOU" DON'T WE UNDERSTAND?

Ever find yourself obsessed with acquiring certain things, or spending lots of time thinking about what you want?

WE CAN EASILY BE TRAPPED INTO:

- seeking things that we really don't need...

- with money we really don't have...

- to impress people we really don't know...

Remember the old (yet still very true) saying: "You can't take it with you," and here's another old saying: "He who has nothing has no worries."

Not long ago, I felt a powerful urge to get rid of the many things I had collected over most of my adult life: vintage toys and Christmas "wish books" from the 1950s and 60s, books about cars (more than 60 of them), trains (more than 20), and antique pedal cars.

I prayed that God would help me in the process of unloading these items, and boy did he! I placed a classified ad selling two of my unrestored 1930s-era pedal cars. I thought I'd start small, knowing I had lots more to sell.

The next day I received many calls, and ultimately a nice young man came over to make the purchase. (I later learned that he was one of the wealthiest people in town!) As he peeled off a wad of $100 bills, he causally asked, "What else have you got?" adding that he collected a wide variety of items, but especially old toys. Over the next four days, he ended up purchasing the entire lot of "stuff" I had amassed over the years.

My prayers had been answered – swiftly and decisively, thanks be to God! And words cannot express the relief I felt that day, to be "free" from the many possessions I was holding onto. You know, when we get whatever "thing" we've been wanting, then what? There is often no place for the energy, enthusiasm and excitement to go. You look for it, you acquire it, and then you store it – because the fun is over.

Part 2

THE PATTERN

Our decisions about life pass through the filter of our beliefs and morals. And what we do, based on those beliefs and morals, reveals the "virtues" in our life. Virtues are personal patterns or habits of good behavior – shining examples of moral excellence and strong character that conform to the standard of the highest good: Jesus Christ. Sent by the Father, he is the pattern for our practice of the virtues. And practicing the virtues is a matter of habit – of choosing to conduct yourself with integrity.

Why are virtues important? They are how we follow Christ in action. Think of his virtuous life as a lighthouse that shines its beam through the fog. That's the kind of life we can model!

When your life journey is unclear, hazy or difficult, the Holy Spirit will guide you, illuminating the path before you. Why? So that day-by-day you will follow Christ, practicing those virtues on your journey to the heavenly Father.

Through the gift of God's grace, three key supernatural virtues are infused within you at baptism:

FAITH - believing in Christ and his truth, placing your life entirely within his care.

HOPE – trusting in Jesus for eternal life; relying on his mercy and the grace given to us by the Holy Spirit.

LOVE – passionately loving God above all else, and loving your neighbor as Christ has loved you. This love, as the Bible tells us, is poured out into our hearts by the Holy Spirit.

These virtues grow stronger or weaker depending on your **actions**.

All other virtues, founded on Christ's love, are acquired by God's grace and through your own efforts, growing stronger or weaker depending on your **actions**. And these virtues lead us to God.

There is a pattern we can follow, that will help us sharpen our virtues, and use the gifts and talents God has given us to their maximum potential. We find that pattern in Christ. In this section, you'll discover many of the virtues that are evident in the lives of others, especially those who follow Christ... virtues like patience, hope and purity.

God gives us these virtues from the abundance of his love. But his gift becomes our task: practice these virtues daily, and you'll grow not only more virtuous, you'll grow more like Christ and more in love with God and neighbor as you cooperate with him in a collaborative partnership.

Chapter 8

PATIENCE

Concrete is incredibly unforgiving. Once you mix it, pour it and let it harden, there's no undoing what you've done. Boy, did I learn that lesson!

I needed to create an 18-inch-deep foundation for a lamppost, which would be secured to it by four bolts set in concrete. After carefully digging the hole and pouring the concrete, I used the manufacturer's template to set the bolts in the wet concrete mix. The next day, I stood the lamppost upright and attempted to secure it to the foundation… only to learn that the bolts had shifted as the concrete had hardened. The bolt pattern no longer matched the holes in the lamppost, and I was forced to unearth a 150-pound chunk of concrete and start all over again. That required a whole lot of patience!

Isn't it good to know that God isn't like that hard, unforgiving concrete? He's always merciful and forgiving, patiently allowing us to repent and re-connect with him despite our failings, sins and shortcomings. No digging required!

Patience is the virtue that allows us to quietly persevere in the face of troubles and provocation. Just think how patient Jesus was, enduring many trials and difficult times. He was willing to persevere through them all because he trusted in God the Father and knew that day-by-day, he would experience the Father's will unfolding.

We all need patience! Patience requires **self-control**. Let's face it – there are certain things in life that drive us crazy and really test our patience: whining children, a flat tire in the parking lot, a broken jar of jam on the kitchen floor, an overflowing toilet (which can be especially embarrassing when you cause it to happen at someone else's house). To stay under control, we often need to muster up as much self-restraint as possible, and that can seem nearly impossible.

Want an exercise in patience? Try going fishing with young children. If you've done this, you know exactly what I mean: tangled lines, snagged lures and hooks that seem destined to catch some part of your body instead of the fish they were meant for. I've even had one of my kids cast the line, rod <u>and</u> reel into the lake! Go fishing with youngsters, and you may not land any fish… but you'll definitely catch a lesson in self-restraint.

Perhaps a better way for us to develop patience is to think of people who display patience, and try to emulate their example (hint: think of your kindergarten teacher).

We never lack in daily opportunities to show patience – whether we are at home, driving, working or shopping. I discovered this a few years ago when my wife was out of town on a ten-day trip, and I had sole responsibility for taking our kids to and from school. One of those mornings, I was running late (as usual) and had to hustle the kids out the door, herd them into the car and race to school at full speed. I was a man on a mission, so single-minded in my purpose that it took my 9-year-old several attempts to get my attention. We were halfway to school before I tuned in to what he was trying to tell me: he had forgotten his shoes! At that point, I had only two choices: either explode in volcano-like eruptions of anger and frustration, or take a deep breath, turn the car around and quietly solve the problem. By God's grace, I chose the second option – and not only learned yet another lesson in patience, but was able to demonstrate it to my kids.

The fruits of practicing the virtue of patience include: less volatility in our relationships, less stress in our life, a greater sense of enduring self-control, and a greater closeness to God. Let Jesus show you how to be more patient. Ask for his help in prayer. He won't let you down.

Chapter 9

HUMILITY

A true car enthusiast never forgets his first restoration project. In my case, it was a 1929 Ford Special Coupe which I completely dismantled and rebuilt from the ground up. At one point, I was tightening the bolts around the transmission case, giving each one a heavy pull on the wrench to ensure maximum tightness. On the very last one, my enthusiasm got the best of me, and I ended up snapping the head clean off the bolt, leaving the threaded remnants buried inside the transmission case.

With a lot of sweat and scraped knuckles, I managed to extract the broken bolt shaft. But more importantly, I learned the value of realizing limitations... and staying within them.

It's easy for us, in our humanness, to exceed our limitations by relying on ourselves more than God. But he never "overtightens" us beyond our limitations; always offering us the grace we need to bear our trials. So instead of trusting in our own strength, let's humble ourselves before God and his grace for all our needs and for all good things.

Are we willing to submit to God's will in such a way that we constantly seek his guidance? Are we willing to collaborate – to truly work with him – so that his plan for our lives can be implemented?

If we are, then we can make a conscious effort to seek God's grace to increase our humility and decrease our pride. Just as the presence of weeds hinders the growth of a fruit tree, the presence of pride defeats the growth of humility. An honest, self-examination may reveal the presence and extent of pride in our lives.

Pride takes many forms: An inflated ego. Retained anger. Sarcasm. Pleasure-seeking. It is the most common and most fundamental vice, and one that challenges us daily. Left unchecked, it can grow to dangerous – even disastrous – proportions.

When my grandmother arrived in the United States, she was barely 20 years old. She spoke only Armenian and knew little about American culture. One day, behind her small Central California farmhouse, my grandmother noticed that a small, green plant had sprung up from the soil. She began to water it daily, and the plant flourished, responding with vigorous growth. Soon it was two feet tall, then four feet, then a towering six feet tall. Finally, a neighbor broke the news to her: the plant she had been watering and nurturing was nothing more than a weed. Embarrassed by her naiveté, she immediately cut it down.

> Are we willing to draw attention away from ourselves and toward God as the source of all good things?

Pride is a lot like that. The more we nourish our ego with "self," the more vigorous the growth of pride. The result? Pride eventually grows to greater and greater heights. But with God's help, we can cut it down, roots and all (especially the roots!).

Are we willing to draw attention away from ourselves and toward God as the source of all good things?

To become more humble, can we empty our egos and give credit to God for all that happens in our life? This includes thanksgiving not just for the good, but also for the struggles and sufferings. Within such trials we can find God, who is ever-present to lighten our burdens.

Humility leads to trust. One of my sons demonstrated incredible, childlike trust at the age of four, when he would routinely leap into our swimming pool and shout "Dad!" while in mid-air. He didn't know how to swim, but he knew I would catch him and hold him above the waterline. Are we willing to trust our Father in the same way?

❧ WILL I BE REMEMBERED FOR MY HUMILITY?

In 1999, I produced a video documentary about St. Joseph that featured several speakers, including evangelist Jesse Romero. A powerful speaker with a dynamic personality, Jesse had several memorable segments – in fact, many people told me that he was their favorite person on the video! A year after releasing the video, I ran into Jesse at a conference and told him how much his comments had touched viewers. His reaction? "All the Glory to God." He drew no attention to himself. Instead, he immediately directed all the praise and positive feedback to our God. Now **that's** humility!

It's tough to be humble in a world focused on personal pride and possessions. We can see the rise of pride all around us, even in the evolution of magazine titles. Through the years, we've gone from *Life* to *People* to *Us* to *Self* – pretty revealing, eh?

With God's help, we can move away from "self" and focus on our relationships with God and others, seeing everything as a gift to be used for the glory of God and the service of others. One of Jesus' most powerful sayings in the Gospel is: "Learn from me, for I am gentle and lowly in heart." (Matthew 11:29)

Chapter 10

SIMPLICITY

I have been a collector since childhood. Stamps and baseball cards at first. Then, as an adult, automobilia, Zorro and Davy Crockett collectibles, antique pedal cars and pre-war Fords. Through the years, I ultimately learned that the "hunt" is more fun than the "capture" – that **seeking** the hard-to-find is more exciting than actually owning it.

But there is another important lesson here that's easy to overlook in the pursuit of "things" – a lesson about simplicity.

Think of those who live simply and modestly – those who don't feel the need to "keep up with the Joneses," but who are content with what they have. Society tends to shun such people, but they have a blessing many Americans will never know: the blessing of an "uncluttered" life. This allows a focus on what brings true meaning and purpose to life.

It's within a simple, ordinary, seemingly mundane life that we can discover daily opportunities for holiness. And become extraordinary in ordinary things.

The ordinary is all around us: doing housework, shopping for groceries, folding clothes, making dinner, driving to work or school. These are all opportunities for grace-filled moments and for listening to the quiet voice of God in our hearts.

In today's culture of activity and accumulation, we all have too much clutter, too many distractions. We allow ourselves to be overbooked, overcommitted and overrun with possessions. I'm talking about a simple life, free from the many distractions that tempt us today. In the simplicity of life, we can find the profound. In ordinary events, we can experience the mystery and the presence of God.

Some years back, my wife and I built our "dream home" – a 4,000 square foot beauty located in an upscale neighborhood. During the year of design and the next year of building, I unwittingly placed greater and greater importance on the house. It was going to be the place where our children would be raised, and where their children would come to visit. It would be a place where memories were made and cherished for generations. From its features to its floorplan to its future, I had it all planned out.

For the first two years, the home lived up to my plans. Then one night as my wife and I returned home from an evening out, we noticed an eerie orange glow in the skies above our neighborhood. From our car windows, we saw that the usually empty streets were lined with cars, onlookers and camera crews from local television stations. Then I saw it – our dream home was engulfed in flames. And all my plans had gone – quite literally – up in smoke.

> How can we eliminate the clutter and distractions from our lives?

It was in that moment that God spoke to me. Not in a voice I could hear, but in the silence of my mind and heart. He reminded me that this house was really no more than a thing – a collection of sticks, bricks and nails – and that I had invested far too much in it.

I was reminded of what really matters: relationships. Those with God, my family and friends. As sometimes happens in our spiritual journey, it was a wake-up call. A call to simplicity.

So how can we eliminate the clutter and distractions from our lives so that we can enjoy the benefits of simplicity? Start small: Look around you right now. Do you see too many books and magazines? Give them away. Too many unnecessary possessions? Sell or donate them. If clutter isn't the problem, look at your lifestyle. Are you involved in too many hobbies, or spending too much time on recreation or entertainment? Cut back.

✿ WHY IS SIMPLICITY IMPORTANT?

Try to take your life from "complex" to "manageable." Then go from "manageable" to "simple." Take small steps. Redefine what you really "need" versus what you "want."

The virtue of simplicity is important not only in our lifestyle, but also in the practice of our faith. I'm talking about a **simple** faith, one that sees God simply as Lord and Giver of life to all. This was powerfully illustrated within a group of Scouts on a weekend campout. Sitting around the fire one night, the leader asked each Scout to say what they're thankful for. One by one, each offered thanks "for my parents," "for these beautiful mountains," "for friends." Then a Scout, blind since birth, took a turn and said, "I'm thankful for being blind." After a long silence, one of the other Scouts asked, "Why are you thankful for that?" The blind Scout answered, "Because the first thing I'll ever see will be the face of my Lord in heaven."

Now that's a simple faith! Simple yet profound, saying more in one comment than a vast library of books could ever communicate about the subject.

Chapter 11

OBEDIENCE

I went on my first out-of-state trip when I was a young man of 18. My destination? The pretty little town of Amarillo, Texas. My purpose? Boot camp! I had just entered the California Air National Guard, and from my first moments in Amarillo I quickly learned the importance of following orders properly. Obedience became a survival skill – doing exactly what I was told, when I was told to do it. Not to anticipate commands, but to wait for the order and respond.

Joseph, the earthly father of Jesus, is one of the all-time great examples of obedience. He gradually came to know God's will, and responded with complete trust, surrender and compliance. For example, when he was told to leave immediately for Egypt with his wife and the baby Jesus, he went. Joseph didn't weigh the options or discuss it with family and friends. He obeyed. He knew what God wanted and he conformed to God's will – a pattern that became a major part of his relationship with the Father.

Can we be like Joseph in that regard? Yes, but it takes consistency; praying daily for the grace to know God's will and respond with complete submission. To do any less is to remain distant from the true joy that occurs when we do what God wants.

The word **obedience** comes from the Latin language: *obaudire*. "Audire" means to listen; *obaudire* means to listen to someone with <u>intent</u> – that is, with the intention to follow their instructions. So obedience always begins by listening to the Holy Spirit. How do we listen? By praying and reading Scripture, and being

❧ How can I listen to God?

ever-attentive to the voice of God in the daily events and circumstances of our lives – listening to discover God's will for our lives, with the intention of following it.

I once had what I considered a world-class headache, the mother of all headaches – a pain so persistent, so oppressive that I went to the hospital to have it checked out. As it turned out, my headache was a symptom of something far more serious: viral meningitis – inflammation of the membrane that covers the brain. Isolated in a quarantine room for two days, I had plenty of time to think and pray. That's when my relationship with God came into clear focus. Placed in a 10-by-10 foot room, lying in a 3-by-6 foot bed, removed from people, possessions and my position in life, I realized just how miniscule I was compared to the cosmos and God's eternal kingdom. And I saw that, ultimately, that's how I might face God – far removed from the world as we know it. Small, humbled and completely accountable for the level of obedience (or disobedience) I have displayed in my life.

The life of Jesus speaks volumes about faithful obedience. If we go to him in prayer and ask for his help, he will instruct us, showing us how to **listen** to God and how to **respond** to what we hear. After all, his mission remains unchanged: to help us discover his self-giving love and the eternal presence of the Father.

> Obedience requires the heart of a child and the mind of a servant.

Obedience requires the heart of a child and the mind of a servant. Servanthood (I don't mean slavery) isn't a bad thing, although to some it may sound as if serving someone (even God) takes away from our freedom. Actually, it's just the opposite – to serve God is an expression of our free will. We freely choose to be at his service and, in so doing, relish in the joy of it all. There is no greater peace, nothing more fulfilling, than serving God through prayer, worship and our relationships with others.

As parents, we are also called to teach obedience to our children. We have daily opportunities for doing this. And in the process of teaching them, they will learn what it means to follow Christ in conforming to the Father's will. Whether we realize it or not, we are often the first experience of God's nature for our children. So, when we are kind, merciful, fair and forgiving, they remember that. And when we are angry, out-of-control, sarcastic or unforgiving, they remember that, too.

We are accountable to God for our actions, especially in our home and family. So let us listen for the voice of Christ, the Good Shepherd, and follow him. And teach our children to do the same.

Chapter 12

PRAYERFULNESS

I grew up building plastic models of just about every kind imaginable, from automobiles to amphibious tanks, airplanes to aircraft carriers. I especially enjoyed painting and detailing model cars, often adding "custom" touches like painted bolt heads and spark plug wires… even using fishing line to simulate fuel lines.

But my customization efforts paled in comparison to those of a young man I met a few years ago. He showed me an ingenious way of putting sound in model cars by using small headphone speakers as seat cushions. The wires from the speakers were then plugged into a music source and sound would boom out of an otherwise ordinary model car!

We're a lot like those models ourselves – each of us needing assembly. God wants to help us with that process, and loves putting his personal touches on the details of our lives. And just as my young friend desired to install a sound system in a model car, God also desires that his voice be heard in our lives through daily Scripture reading and prayer. His Word – his "broadcast" – then becomes an integrated part of who we are and what we do, a soundtrack for our spiritual journey.

And we have the incredible privilege of being able to tune into that broadcast every day. To be deeply immersed in God's Word. To discover and follow Christ in fulfilling the Father's will. To **listen** to God in Scripture and to **speak** with God in prayer.

There are times when the best way to "tune in" to God is through **prayer** without words. In the sanctuary of silence, we can experience the presence of God in our minds and hearts. Words can be distracting, but silence helps us to listen.

Spiritual growth occurs when we pray and read the Bible regularly... daily. Go ahead and schedule a "prayer appointment" in your daily planner, if it will help you set aside time for this. Or you may prefer to pray first thing in the morning or last thing each evening (or both!). Whatever time you choose, do it consistently. Every day.

And pray with your family, too. I realized some years back that the only time my family prayed together was at dinner – grace – a total of **seven seconds!** Well, we changed that and now have family prayers each evening.

> Course corrections are necessary for our spiritual journey.

Through Scripture reading and prayer, the Holy Spirit keeps us on course as we make our earthly pilgrimage to the heavenly Father. If you've ever been on a long international flight, you probably noticed that the airline provides an electronic world map on the plane's monitors, with a red line showing the plane's progress between your points of departure and arrival. But what the monitors don't show are the many course corrections employed throughout your flight. Most commercial jets are actually "off course" most of the time – but don't be alarmed! The pilot constantly makes course corrections to keep the plane on its flight plan. We do the same thing on a smaller scale when we "nudge" the steering wheel while traveling down the road. If we fail to make adjustments and corrections while driving, we may end up off the road and, ultimately, in the hospital or the cemetery.

Course corrections – made through a strong spiritual life, fortified by daily Scripture reading and prayer – are necessary for our spiritual journey as well. Just as conversation is the best way to get to know someone, prayer is the best way to get to know and love the Father, Son and the Holy Spirit. But it's important that we understand our part in their divine conversation. I learned that lesson some years back, when I was distressed about a less-than-satisfying relationship with a family

❧ WHY IS PRAYER IMPORTANT?

member. I told God about the problem in prayer, and asked him to bring harmony between my relative and myself, but nothing changed even after weeks of prayer. The relationship remained distant and cold.

Then I learned why God had allowed the problem to continue: in my prayers, I was not only giving God the problem, but also telling him the solution! I had to recognize the importance of letting God come up with the solution, rather than treating him like a heavenly vending machine. I learned to trust him for the answer according to his will. And once I did that, I was at peace.

Chapter 13

FAITHFULNESS

In 1988, a massive earthquake struck Armenia, the country where many of my ancestors lived. It was devastating. Over 25,000 people were killed in the blink of an eye. Within minutes of the quake, a father rushed to his son's school and his worst nightmare was confirmed: the building had been reduced to a pile of debris. The father had promised his son that he would always be there for him and, driven by this commitment, he began digging through the rubble. Other parents had given up any hope of finding their children alive, but the father kept digging. Brick by brick, stone by stone, he dug for the rest of the day and into the night.

By morning, he still had not found his son, but undeterred, he kept digging with calloused hands and bleeding fingers all through the next day and night. Then, forty hours into his search, the father removed a boulder and heard something he feared he would never hear again: his son's voice! When he called the boy's name, he answered, "It's me, father! I told the others not to worry, that if you were alive, you would save us. I remembered your promise that you would always be there for me."

That's the kind of faith we see in the lives of those who put their trust fully and completely in God. Nothing can interfere with their beliefs and commitment. In turn, God is faithful, providing the grace and blessings needed to fulfill each believer's vocation and mission.

A deep, profound faith leads us to love God for who he is, rather than for just what he can do for us. As we are given the gift of faith, it becomes our responsibility to live it and share it with others – to let the light of Christ and his truth reflect through us and illuminate the dark world around us.

On a missionary trip to China, an eye surgeon helped a man, nearly blind by cataracts, recover his eyesight. Weeks later, the doctor was surprised to find 40 other blind men seeking his help. They had walked over 250 miles through some of the most rugged and remote countryside in order to ask the doctor to restore their sight. When the doctor asked how they had made the difficult journey, the men explained that they had all held a rope that kept them together. At the front of the rope, leading the way, was the man who had his eyesight restored by the surgeon.

The man had been given the gift of sight, and he immediately wanted to share it with others. In the same way, when we are given the gift of faith, we'll want to share it! To ensure that our faith remains strong and growing, we can nurture it – through prayer, Bible reading, community worship and holding fast to an abiding certainty that God will provide for our needs. In fact, God knows much more about what we truly need than we do!

It is particularly within our struggles and brokenness that faith is so vitally important. I remember jogging one afternoon alongside my 7-year-old son, who was riding his bicycle. As we neared home, he raced ahead of me until he came to a fairly steep hill. It didn't take me long to catch up with him, as he was pedaling slower and slower, huffing and puffing with exertion and frustration. I placed my hand on his backside and helped him pedal to the top of the hill. That was years ago, but I have often thought of the metaphor there... how God comes to our aid during the uphill struggles we face.

Still, there are situations in life that seem utterly hopeless, in which God seems distant and our faith is tested. My father died just before my sixteenth birthday. It was a time of deep doubt and confusion for me: after all, how could God let such a good man – a devoted husband and loving father – die? Even now, I still don't have all the answers. But I do know that God is real. He never left my father's side. He loved my dad completely, and loves me completely. That's what faith is all about: believing when you don't fully understand.

Chapter 14

HUMOR

It happened in a fancy French restaurant in downtown San Francisco. I had just been seated with two rehabilitation nurses who worked with me professionally on injury cases – three colleagues all dressed up and anticipating a pleasant get-together. As we waited to place our order, the nurse next to me buttered a slice of bread and began telling us a story about her daughter, using gestures that became more animated as the story went on. Suddenly, while punctuating the climax of her story, the piece of bread flew from her hand, shot across the table, hit the other nurse on her right cheek… and stuck there! (Yet another danger of using too much butter.)

Believe it or not, this situation isn't covered in the etiquette books. What was the "gentlemanly" thing to do? Reach across the table and peel the bread off her face? Offer her my napkin? Stick bread on <u>my</u> face? I was at a loss.

Fortunately, after a moment of awkward silence, we all enjoyed a hearty laugh. That moment couldn't have been more comically perfect if it had been planned and rehearsed. It was funny – truly funny.

No doubt about it, humor is something we all need. (Especially the upscale diners and snooty waiter who looked down their noses at us as we guffawed loudly.)

Humor is a great device to be modeled in our own homes – not necessarily by creating an atmosphere of non-stop jokes and pratfalls, but in a way that encourages laughter without hurting others. Today's brand of popular humor is often rooted in sarcasm – cutting remarks meant to demean someone else. That kind of humor hurts, and has no place in our relationships with others.

Years ago, I was the featured speaker at the local chapter of a national service club. The fellow who introduced me to the audience thought he was being funny when he said, "As I bring Rick up to the podium, the words of John Wayne come to mind: 'The only good Armenian is a dead Armenian.'" (Of course, John Wayne never said this.) As someone of Armenian heritage, I found the "joke" to be in incredibly poor taste. Especially since 1.5 million Armenians were killed in massacres between 1915-1923. I almost walked out – and looking back, I wish I had.

The point? We've got to be careful about our jokes and the subject matter. It can't be too difficult, since there is so much truly humorous "clean" material to laugh about in our daily lives. Material that brings about cheerfulness and joy.

Humor can also help us deal with situations that are annoying, frustrating or upsetting, even embarrassing. Try laughing at them next time. After all, we do have a choice how we react – we can either lighten up or let things weigh us down. Let's choose to lighten up, and see if our problems are still as big as we think they are!

A classic example happened in my home several years ago. I was reaching across the breakfast table with a full half-gallon of milk, attempting to pour it into a cup for one of my kids. The slippery carton dropped out of my hand, landed on its side and proceeded to cover the table in a flood of milk. The scene seemed to unfold in slow motion, as we were momentarily paralyzed by the hypnotic "glug-glug-glug" of escaping milk. By the time our brains had processed what had transpired, the carton was nearly empty. I saw the humor in the situation and we all shared a good laugh. (Not to mention a milkless breakfast.) To this day, "The Great Milk Spill By Dad" remains a treasured family story.

Need a good laugh? Look back on embarrassing moments in your life, and enjoy a laugh at your own expense. It works for me! If you can laugh at yourself, you probably have pride under control… and that's good! God still loves us even when we've goofed up.

Chapter 15

STRENGTH

It was a dark and stormy night. (Sounds like the opening line of a bad novel, doesn't it?) I was traveling across the San Mateo Bridge to visit my brother in the San Francisco Bay area. The storm was intense – pounding rain, howling winds, almost zero visibility – and the traffic was heavy.

The narrow bridge was little more than a stretch of roadway running barely above the water of the bay, and that night the dark, churning ocean waves seemed to be grasping for my car, ready to pull me off the bridge and drag me down into the icy depths below. I have to admit, I was frightened. I prayed fervently, and I knew I had to "brave it out" – after all, with so much traffic around me, what choice did I have but to continue moving forward? After a few miles, the roadway rose to a higher bridge span, and the ocean's threat steadily diminished until finally I was driving on solid ground.

We are each called upon to be brave in different ways and at different times. My own father had a lot to teach me about bravery, strength and toughness.

He was strong in the face of adversity and the difficult economy of his time – a strength he found in God's mantle of grace that covered his family. He was also rugged and physically strong. My father **had** to be in his line of work as a big-rig driver and heavy truck mechanic – demanding jobs for a young man, but ones he handled with great skill.

His greatest challenge came one afternoon on California's notorious "Ridge Route" – a steep, harrowing descent from a high mountain range into the valley below. The Ridge Route tested the mettle of every driver, but particularly big-rig truck drivers whose tons of cargo propelled them down the grade with frightening momentum. My dad had just begun his descent when he came to the sudden, sickening realization that he had lost his brakes. He and his 70,000 pounds of rolling freight were out of control.

> Surviving life's storms sometimes requires supernatural strength.

As news of dad's runaway truck quickly spread, police units were called to act as safety escorts, but they couldn't keep up. Terrified motorists cleared a path for dad's truck, which careened crazily around curves and gained deadly momentum on the straightaways. By God's grace, my dad was able to stay on the road as the Ridge Route gradually leveled off into the valley floor, and the truck eventually rolled to a safe stop. Exhausted from the sheer stress of his ordeal, my dad passed out. But he survived, thanks to his strength – not just his physical strength, but more importantly, the strength of his resolve as he fully devoted his energies to keeping himself and others from tremendous potential harm.

That's the kind of personal resolve it takes to defend ourselves and our families from moral and spiritual injury. To demonstrate fortitude in situations that trouble or endanger us – whether it's spiritual attack, physical harm, illness, temptation, difficult relationships or habitual sin. Through the virtues of strength and fortitude, our "staying power" can get us through whatever difficulties we face.

That's pictured powerfully in the Chinese bamboo tree, which only appears to grow an inch or two during its first four years. But in its fifth year, the bamboo shoots up to heights of 60 feet or more. What's going on in those first four years? The bamboo is growing like crazy, but not above ground where it can be seen. In fact, its roots are spreading far and deep into the earth, providing a strong anchor for the height that will follow. Similarly, to be firmly rooted in Christ means we are well-anchored when the world tries to pull us down or the storms of life threaten to blow us over.

✤ HOW CAN I PERSEVERE IN DIFFICULT TIMES?

Surviving life's storms sometimes requires supernatural strength. This was brought home to me in the summer of 1969, when I was stationed in Gulfport, Mississippi for training with my California Air National Guard unit. Little did we know that within days of our arrival, we would be tested not by an enemy or military action, but by the primitive power and unleashed fury of Hurricane Camille.

Camille struck in the dead of night, while we took shelter in barracks made of concrete block and wood. The screeching wind ripped the roof right off our building, exposing us to torrents of rain from the skies above and a parade of snakes seeking higher ground from the swamps below. Many of us sandwiched ourselves between mattresses for protection from flying debris. While I'd like to tell you I was calm in the face of danger, I'd be lying – I was terrified! But God gave me the inner strength and fortitude to ride the storm out. When it was all over, our camp looked like a war zone after heavy shelling. Thanks be to God, we were all safe and accounted for, but 256 others in Mississippi and Louisiana lost their lives to Hurricane Camille.

Strength is a curious human quality: it involves more than mere muscle power, and includes the mind and spirit as well. To grow stronger in any of these areas, a combination of exercise and nutrition is required.

After being a runner for over 30 years, I decided to add weight lifting to my weekly exercise regime. I thought I was in shape, but boy was I wrong! While my cardiopulmonary system was fit from running, I had grossly neglected muscle maintenance and so began the tedious process of strength training and making drastic changes in my diet. I learned from a trainer that if I wanted to improve my muscle tone or size, I had to support my exercise program with the right combination of protein, fat and carbohydrates.

The same holds true for our mind and spirit when, through prayer and Scripture reading, we obtain strength for ourselves in these areas. That's the kind of exercise and nutrition program that delivers a big spiritual payoff... the ultimate "diet" plan.

As men and women of faith, it's important that we remain strong in body, mind and spirit. That's because God calls us to be "counter-cultural," going against the grain of a worldly culture that promises short-lived pleasure rather than long-lasting joy.

God calls us to be brave, even fearless; unyielding to the pressure of the secular world that surrounds us. Our dedication is to the person of Jesus Christ, as our "personal trainer," who gives us the grace and **courage** to abide in him.

Chapter 16

KINDNESS

Fred Rogers was best known to generations of TV as the beloved host of "Mr. Rogers' Neighborhood." I think what appealed to adults and children alike was his pleasant nature – he always appeared to be kind, thoughtful and full of good will. Many who knew him well have said there was no difference between his on-camera persona and his off-camera persona. He was consistently calm and kind, whether or not the camera was rolling.

While intended for children, "Mr. Rogers' Neighborhood" was among my favorite shows to watch after a tough day at work. How could I stay upset when Mr. Rogers posed thought-provoking questions like, "Do puppies sleep in pup-tents?" He was a one-of-a-kind fellow – creative, considerate and cooperative with others.

But Fred Rogers didn't have a corner on the kindness market. In a profound way, Mother Teresa of Calcutta personified kindness in her work with "the poorest of the poor." Along with her religious congregation (aptly named "Missionaries of Charity"), she unceasingly assisted the forgotten, sick and dying in the name of Christ's love and kindness. Her unselfish life was marked by true thoughtfulness, deep understanding and good deeds.

Being consistently kind means going out of ourselves, leaving our "comfort zone," overcoming our self-centeredness. Ask yourself: if you died today, would people

✤ ARE YOU KNOWN FOR YOUR KINDNESS?

remember you as a **kind** person? Would they talk about your kindness at your funeral? Could they give examples of your acts of kindness? Can **you**, right now?

If you want to grow in this virtue, look for examples of kindness in others. I found a great example in one of my sons. He has been a faithful friend to a boy who was born without the lower portions of his legs, fully accepting the boy's limitations. He doesn't treat him as someone fragile or impaired. Through his attitude of kindness, my son takes the "dis" out of "disability," placing value on what his friend **can** do rather than what he **can't** do. (Wearing prosthetic legs, the young lad is able to play basketball and flag football!)

> Showing kindness gets easier the more you do it.

How often do we adults fail to accept someone because of his or her flaws and failings? Many turn quickly away from the imperfections of humanity; they have no time for tolerance, goodwill or positive regard. As my son accepts his young friend, so Jesus accepts each and every one of us, with all of our flaws. We are called to be the image of Christ to others, to reflect his light: his compassion, concern and kindness to all God's creatures.

Think of someone right now that tries your kindness. Don't settle for someone "easy," but think of someone to whom it would seem impossible for you to be kind. Now make a diligent effort to be kind to that person for seven days. Make him or her your "project" for the coming week. You might want to follow the philosophy of the Boy Scout slogan: "Do a Good Turn Daily," looking actively for opportunities to spontaneously help others in need with the hand of kindness. I think you'll find that showing kindness gets easier the more you do it, just like exercise or weight training. Practice makes perfect!

In situations where we can't directly intervene with kindness, we can do so indirectly through prayer and charitable contributions. Every time we pray for another person, it's kindness. Giving money to a relief organization is kindness.

Donating clothing and household items to a charity is kindness. So look for different ways to express kindness in the world around you. To be **tolerant** with other people, **understanding** when there is a change of plans and **thoughtful** in recognizing the needs of others.

Lastly, let your kindness be genuine, not phony – consistent, not just convenient.

A friend told me about a homeless fellow who approached him as he was having lunch outdoors. The man asked for some milk to settle his stomach. My friend promptly gave him a dollar, but later realized that he did so only to be rid of him. He didn't want his lunch interrupted. The genuinely kind (and Christ-like) response would have been to buy the man some milk and even stay with him as he drank it. The homeless are often in great need of human contact, especially in the form of conversation.

Chapter 17

PURITY

I was at the checkout counter of a large retail chain store with one of my sons, then age 14. As usual, a rack of tabloid magazines was prominently on display. But this particular display was unusually offensive, graphic in both word and picture. I'm not talking about idle Hollywood gossip or aliens abducting Elvis, but content that was extraordinarily perverse and explicit. I immediately called for the manager, who listened as I registered my objections. I explained that I was trying to foster an environment for my family that was free from moral assaults. I knew my children would eventually be exposed to such a culture, but I didn't expect it to happen at the checkout of a supposedly "family-friendly" national retailer. To my surprise, the manager not only agreed with my concerns, but removed all copies of the tabloid in question! A small battle was won, but the war wages on. By the following week, more offensive tabloids were on display.

The virtue of purity carries with it the requirement of modesty in our thoughts, words, behavior and dress. If we remain pure, we will be free from moral fault. We will become innocent – a wonderful concept that ought to be treasured, yet is ridiculed by the secular world around us. Another type of modesty maintains a moderate image of ourselves as people who know their limitations, and their need for God's grace.

With God's grace, we will prevail in the battle for purity. Make no mistake, it won't be easy. Every day, we are faced with a steady onslaught of flesh, sexual innuendo and all forms of immorality. Remaining pure is a huge challenge, as we attempt to "swim" through the sewage dumped on us daily from titillating television programs and movies, slick magazines and the seemingly bottomless cesspool of pornographic websites. It takes regular, daily prayer for the strength to control our thoughts and desires.

In the Beatitudes (see Matthew 5), Jesus tells us that the "pure in heart" are blessed for they shall see God. This is our real yearning: for God. All the beauty and pleasure of this created world cannot satisfy our desire to see God himself. Impurity clouds this vision and can eternally rob us of it.

Mastering our thoughts is one of the most difficult challenges in our human nature. Rev. John Hardon taught that:

> THOUGHTS lead to desires.
>
> DESIRES lead to actions.
>
> ACTIONS lead to habits.
>
> HABITS shape our character.
>
> CHARACTER determines our destiny.
>
> And it all begins in the MIND.

We can't let our guard down. (Though we do.) Temptation and sins of the flesh swarm around us like flies at a summer barbecue. Self-mastery is an apprenticeship that never ends. As one elderly fellow told me, "Temptation won't stop until 30 minutes or so after you die."

And if we do fall, let's not fall into despair. Then is the time to turn to Christ for forgiveness, for pardon and peace. Then is the time to start afresh, again!

Parents can look to God for fatherly guidance in practicing the virtues of purity, modesty and chastity, and in the proper ways to raise our children and keep them

✦ AM I PURE IN HEART?

(and ourselves!) morally straight. I have had talks and on-site "field trips" with my kids on the subject of bad magazines, bad CDs, bad movies and bad language. I've told them the bad words they are sure to hear and what these words mean. Let me tell you, it wasn't easy doing this with them in their innocence and youth. But parents can equip their children with the skills and tools that will help them face adulthood with confidence, integrity and high moral values. We can teach this through the use of Scripture, daily prayer and good stories. It's strong medicine – but then again, we're fighting a powerful, out-of-control disease. And if we don't teach them, by default, the world will.

Chapter 18

COMMITMENT

We are surrounded by committed people: Athletes committed to their sport. Soldiers committed to their mission. Singers committed to their music. Teachers committed to their students. Doctors committed to their patients.

Can we be committed to an interior life of prayer and spiritual growth – to the hidden life, calling no undue attention to ourselves? Are we willing to forgo recognition? (I love what President Harry Truman once said: "It is amazing what you can accomplish if you do not care who gets the credit.") Are we willing to let go of our egos? Place no importance on possessions? Make Scripture, prayer and interior growth our highest spiritual priorities?

Of course, the greatest story ever told – the story of Jesus – is the story of the greatest commitment ever seen. In self-giving love, he was totally commited to the Father when he obediently endured suffering and death on the cross, for us and for our salvation.

Yes, that's what real commitment is all about. Yet, sadly, it is seldom achieved or aimed for. Remember the movie *Mr. Holland's Opus*, about the school teacher whose passion for music came at the expense of his deaf son? Mr. Holland certainly demonstrated commitment in one area, but while he touched the lives of many students, his family relationships suffered. He didn't fulfill his **primary** commitment and mission as a husband and father.

By contrast, we have the amazing opportunity to daily demonstrate our commitment to work, family and faith. Remaining steadfast in our focus on God. Working as an expression of love for God and our family. Creating an atmosphere in the home that leads our children to grow into compassionate, responsible adults. All the while seeking holiness in the "ordinariness" of daily life.

Also, our interior life becomes all the more vibrant with **fasting** – not just abstaining from food, but from other legitimate pleasures in life as well – such as television, movies, magazines, recreation – and, of course, especially sin… and anything that places our focus on self and our own satisfaction, instead of on God. And for those with difficulty controlling your temper, try giving up your anger for a month in the spirit of fasting.

> Prudence is the middle ground between timidity and foolhardiness.

I'll never forget the Lenten season (the forty days leading up to Easter) in which I gave up coffee – no easy task for someone who considers coffee to be far more than just a beverage, but a source of comfort akin to a warm blanket! My first week of Lent included withdrawals, headaches, lethargy and other ills. I would love to tell you that by Easter Sunday, I had kicked the coffee habit for good, but I would be lying. Truth is, I was ready to guzzle the brew straight from the carafe! But I survived. And I look back on that Lenten season as an exercise in commitment. Fasting symbolizes "fasting from sin," so it strengthens us in our resolve to avoid all sin and follow Christ in our daily life.

Thomas Aquinas, a 13th century philosopher and theologian, described the virtue of prudence as "right reason in action" – choosing to do what our conscience and moral reason tells us to do. Prudence is living in the truth. If we act like we have our own "truth," then we are acting against prudence. We become **imprudent**.

The virtue of prudence is linked to the virtue of humility. It's seen in those who don't try to be **more** than they are, nor any **less** than they are. Prudence is the middle ground between timidity and foolhardiness.

I think one of the greatest challenges we have as parents is reasoning with our teenage children. Let's face it: we wonder sometimes when – or even if – they will

❧ How can I be closer to God?

ever arrive at the "age of reason." We're amazed at the logic – or lack thereof – of their arguments and defenses.

Take my teenage sons... please! Now, don't get me wrong – I love my boys, but sometimes I wonder if the hot Central California summers have overheated their logic circuits. In this climate, driving in the car requires the non-stop use of the air-conditioner. It's not an option – it's a fact of life during our 100+ degree summers. Yet my sons will often argue that it's actually "cooler" driving with the windows down. They say that with the wind – hot as it is – blowing on their faces, they "feel" cooler than they do in the gentle currents of the air conditioner. I've tried reasoning, I've tried ranting, but all of my arguments have fallen on deaf (and hot!) ears.

I've come to realize the importance of choosing which battles to fight and which to avoid. And try to distinguish between truth, opinion and prejudice!

There are many in this day and age that have a remarkable interior spirituality – a genuine peace of mind, soul and heart. They've made a commitment. In life's burdens, Christ is the bridge to our heavenly Father. Make a commitment to focus your interior life around Christ and his kingdom. And strengthen your spiritual life through community worship, daily prayer and reading the Bible.

Chapter 19

HOPE

I'll never forget my first running event: a 10K loop through our downtown area. I was only mildly confident I would make it to the finish. I had been running a scant six months, going from "out of shape" to "somewhat improved shape," but nowhere close to what I would consider "10K running shape." As the crowd of runners started off, I had only one goal: making it across the finish line.

That goal was challenged right from the outset, as fast runners whizzed past me at a sub-seven-minute-mile pace. An obese man chugged past me, never letting up from the pounding rhythm of his heavy steps. There was even a runner that finished the event so early, he passed me running in the opposite direction back to the starting line! At long last, I finally did make it across the finish line… thanks to equal amounts of lung power, leg power and lasting hope.

But there is another kind of hope – not in ourselves, but hope in Christ – trusting in him to obtain the kingdom of heaven and eternal life. Hope is rooted in Christ and his promises. And it requires us to rely not on our own strength, but on the grace of the Holy Spirit.

The Holy Spirit guides us how to pray in hope. As we do so, God nourishes this virtue so that it grows in us. As our hope increases, our anxiety decreases. While hope is the confident trust in Christ and his promises, it also carries with it the fear of the Lord: fear of offending God's goodness and love and incurring his just punishments.

Sins against hope occur when we give in to despair or fail to trust in God's mercy and forgiveness – or when we start presuming that we will obtain eternal life through our own merits.

We rely with confidence on God. He is always with us in troubled times – even when we don't always recognize it – in illness, difficult relationships, emergencies, emotional problems… and even in our dying moments.

In my profession, I have seen many cases where traumatic head injuries result in permanent brain damage. These often involve children. My heart goes out to these kids and their parents since the residual effects may include developmental delay, coordination problems and impairments in speech, memory, problem-solving and judgment.

> We rely with confidence on God. He is always with us.

You might tend to think the parents would lapse into hopelessness. But I've found the opposite to be true – often times, they are living examples of hope! They hope for improvement, for their children to return as close as possible to "normal." In particular, many parents often display a steadfast hope that God will faithfully make all things new, and bring blessings into the difficult situations they face. Even with today's amazing medical advances, we are ultimately in God's hands and these families know it. They have been a huge inspiration to me.

In the military, I learned the importance of weaponry to protect myself and safeguard my fellow soldiers. Weapons not only repel attack, but also take the offense against impending danger. Likewise, hope is also a weapon that protects us in our struggle for salvation.

As a vocational rehabilitation consultant, I've had to become familiar with literally thousands of jobs and their requirements. And I've found one occupation that stands above the rest in terms of the knowledge, decision-making ability, life-and-death skills and stress involved. Know what it is? Not an emergency room physician, air traffic controller or law enforcement officer. It's the carrier-based fighter pilot. Having met several of them over the years, I've become immensely impressed with the precise, ultra-vigilant attention they display in order to fulfill their mission.

❧ HOW CAN I BE MORE HOPEFUL?

The fighter pilot is brutally catapulted from the carrier deck, accelerating from zero to 165 miles per hour in less than two seconds! But it's the landing that is most impressive. The pilot intends to hit the carrier deck at precisely the right location, angle and speed to snag one of four arresting cables with the tailhook. Doing this on a carrier that is moving forward, pitching up and down over a windy sea, with a landing deck that doesn't line up with the carrier's direction of movement, is incredibly difficult. Add darkness or bad weather, and you've got the ultimate white-knuckle experience! But with assistance from radar, guidance systems and the carrier crew, fighter pilots successfully accomplish this superhuman challenge on a daily basis.

Our hope in God is much like this. Our goal is to "land" safely in God's eternal kingdom, relying on his "guidance system" of faith, hope and love. Challenging? Yes. Attainable? With his grace, absolutely!

Part 3

THE PLAN

Earlier in this book, I shared the story of the blind man who had been healed, only to return to the physician with 40 other blind men. A tremendous illustration of gratitude and faith, to be sure. But what if you were blind and listening to this man describe his restored eyesight. Would you **believe** him? More importantly, would you **demonstrate** your belief by allowing him to guide you by rope through 250 miles of rugged terrain? Ah! Belief isn't so easy now, is it? But all the belief in the world is useless if you don't take that "next step" and put your belief into **action**.

It's my hope that, by this point in the book, you've moved from just "considering" that God exists to **believing** that he created you, loves you, has a plan for you and wants a close relationship with you. If you do believe, I'm going to ask you to take the "next step" and put your belief into **action**. (No, I'm not going to lead you into the rocky wilderness!) As Christ tells us in the Gospel of Matthew, when we listen to the Word of God and put it into **action**, we are truly building our house on **solid rock** to withstand life's storms (see Matthew 7:24-27).

If you're not ready to make a commitment… to believe that God is real (and madly in love with you!) – that's OK. Keep reading anyway; just allow yourself to be open to God's presence. You may find something in this section that "tips the scale" in favor of believing!

The friendships we make during difficult times, tested and strengthened through trying moments, often last for a lifetime. Such is the case of my friendship with Richard, who I met in one of the most traumatic periods of my life: boot camp!

After a gut-wrenching flight aboard a C-119 cargo plane, a series of immunizations and the most humiliating haircuts of our lives, Richard and I found ourselves in line for clothing issue. First, the issuing officer gave each man in line a three-pack of boxer shorts and ordered us to put on one pair. Next, he threw three-packs of t-shirts at our feet and screamed at us to put one on. So far, so good.

Discovering and following God's will: listen, understand and act.

Then the officer barked an order that didn't seem to make sense: "Put your shirts in your drawers!" Richard and I were paralyzed with bewilderment, struggling to make sense of the order, as the red-faced officer marched over to us and repeated loudly, "Put your shirts in your drawers!" Maybe it was the intimidation, or perhaps the slow process of decoding the officer's order into everyday English, but as it dawned on Richard that we were being ordered to tuck our shirts into our shorts, he took the order literally – very literally – and picked up the plastic bag containing the remaining two shirts, and stuffed it into his shorts. He wasn't trying to be funny – he seriously believed that was what the officer wanted! Turning to me, the officer shrieked in disbelief, "Did you see what he did?" Still intimidated, I obediently said "Yes, Sir!" and immediately placed my pack of shirts inside my boxers.

Looking back, I see both humor and a vital life-lesson here. It's about deeply listening, clearly understanding and taking right action based on the message. Discovering and following God's will is a lot like that: listen, understand and act.

If you believe there is a unique plan for your life – a personal vocation and mission that you alone can fulfill – it's time to start planning your life so that it is in **alignment** with your God-given purpose. In other words, it's time you became familiar with the **Personal Mission Statement**....

DEFINE YOUR MISSION

Bill Havens was chosen to represent the United States in a canoe racing event in the 1924 Summer Olympics in Paris – a once-in-a-lifetime honor that also led to a serious dilemma: his wife was expecting their first child, and was due to give birth during the games. Bill had to decide whether to participate in the event and miss the birth of his first child, or withdraw from the competition and miss the event for which he had trained so intensely. Despite the overwhelming outside pressure to compete in the games, Bill chose to remain behind in order to be there when his son – Frank – was born on August 1, 1924.

A heartwarming story, but that's not the end of it. Twenty-eight years later, during the 1952 Summer Olympics in Helsinki, Bill received this telegram:

> *Dear Dad,*
>
> *Thanks for waiting around for me to get born in 1924.*
> *I'm coming home with the gold medal you should have won.*
>
> *Your loving son,*
> *Frank*

Bill Havens traded what most considered the opportunity of a lifetime for the **real** opportunity of a lifetime. And he left us with a powerful illustration of staying "on course" along life's journey. He knew what was really important, and traded fame for fatherhood. While competing was his passion, fatherhood was his **mission**.

The lesson? If you don't define your mission in life, the world will.

Now it's time to bring things into sharper focus by completing your **Personal Mission Statement**. Don't worry – completing this section doesn't set your mission in stone. In fact, your **Personal Mission Statement** is really never "finished" – it is something you revisit and modify as often as needed through the years ahead. Remember, God probably won't reveal his purpose for you in one cosmic "brain dump." Instead, he will likely reveal it a little at a time, through the course of your lifetime – which means your mission statement may change from time to time, as you learn more about God's unfolding plan and purpose for your life.

Personal Mission Statement

In the grid below, write down how you can serve God in your thoughts, words and actions in settings that include your home, church and world. Your responses will form the basis for your **Personal Mission Statement**.

PERSONAL MISSION STATEMENT GRID
HOME (FAMILY, FRIENDS, OTHER RELATIONSHIPS)
_____
_____
_____
CHURCH (WORSHIP, SERVICE TO OTHERS)
_____
_____
_____
WORLD (WORKPLACE, LOCAL COMMUNITY & SOCIETY IN GENERAL)
_____
_____
_____

Now, take your responses and flesh them out into complete thoughts and sentences (you may want to use a computer so you can save and modify your responses as needed in the coming years). Begin your statement with something like, "GOD'S purpose for my life is..." and complete the statement with your fully-formed responses.

But don't let that be the end of your **Personal Mission Statement!** Set aside a specific block of time each week to review it, as you consider your skills, virtues, gifts, interests and choices. Guided by the Holy Spirit, let it serve as a navigational tool to help you stay on course to our true home with the Father in heaven. Make changes as needed, as you collaborate with Christ in becoming the person he wants you to be. Remember, God loves you completely and without reservation. Trust in him. Press on! Even when you fail or fall short, remember the Lord is there to forgive you and to lift you up from despair, disappointment or depression. Turn to him in your failures and start afresh. Forward then!

Family Mission Statement

God could have created humanity as simply a random collection of lone individuals, each striving to fulfill his or her unique purpose in life. **But he didn't.** He created us with a strong sense of personal connection, of belonging, fostered especially in the family unit. Each of us is born into a family, intended by our Father to be a place of safety, security, nurturing and love. God desires each family to be a community of life and love, responsible for guarding, revealing and communicating love – a reflection of our Father's love for his children.

Sadly, in today's world, many families have wandered far from this purpose: Infidelity. Separation. Divorce. Desertion. Domestic violence. Abuse. They all serve to weaken, and ultimately to fracture, the bonds of family. This has allowed the world to create its own definition of what makes a "family" – a definition that sometimes seems a far cry from the center of love and nurturing that God intended it to be.

Still, there's hope for families that want to remain strong, intact and unified in reflecting God's original plan. Just as God has a unique and unrepeatable purpose for every individual, he also has a special mission for every family. And just as your **Personal Mission Statement** helps you focus on fulfilling your individual mission, your **Family Mission Statement** will help your family – as a whole – fulfill its unique purpose. Here's a simple, 4-step process for creating a **Family Mission Statement**:

STEP 1: DEFINE THE CURRENT STATE OF YOUR FAMILY

Take a good look at what your family is like right now. It may not perfectly reflect God's plan for the family unit, but it will give you a "baseline reading," showing you the areas that need work. Make sure all family members are present, and discuss questions such as:

- What kind of family are we?

- What do we enjoy doing together?

- When do we get along best?

- What is most important to each family member?

- How do we express ourselves spiritually as a family?

- How do we show love to the community around us?

- Do we each have specific responsibilities in the home?

- For each person: what do you like most about our family? Like least?

- What are the special talents and abilities present in each of us?

Have these family discussions regularly (perhaps weekly) and take notes on the answers that are generated. You may have a "snapshot" of your family's current state in just one or two meetings, or it may take several weeks to get to that point. Don't rush this step – the important thing is to keep talking as a family, fostering good communication in a spirit of openness and support.

STEP 2: PLANNING YOUR FAMILY MISSION STATEMENT

How can **your** family, in all its uniqueness and with its one-of-a-kind blend of gifts and talents, fulfill God's purpose as a community of life and love? That answer will be different for every family. In essence, your answer will be your **Family Mission Statement**. How do you arrive at that answer? This step will help you.

Think of your **Family Mission Statement** as a "road map." To make the best use of a road map, you determine where you're starting from (which you learned in the first step, defining the current state of your family) and where you're going. What is God calling you to accomplish as a family? How does God want you to relate to the community around you? As you continue meeting together for family discussions, shift your emphasis to questions such as:

- What does God want of us **right now**?

- What does he want us to **be** and **do**?

- How can we be more loving to each other?

- How can we be more Christ-like to each other? To our community?

- How does God want us to serve the community around us?

- What virtues are most important to our family (such as faith, hope, love, kindness, compassion, sacrifice, courtesy)?

- How can our family address problems or difficulties?

- How can we pray together as a family?

- What is our family's vision for the future in our home? In society?

Family discussions can be an exciting time for coming together in new ways, looking at where you've been, where you are and where God want you to be. Good communication and a shared vision will give your family a firm foundation on which to build a life together. If you like, use the following worksheet to stimulate effective family discussions.

FAMILY MISSION STATEMENT WORKSHEET

1. The virtues that symbolize our family are:

   _____

2. What phase or single word describes our family as God wants us to be?

   _____

3. What is most important to our family?

   _____

4. What is our family's vision for the future in our
   a. Home _____
   b. Church _____
   c. Society _____

5. What family activities are most important to us?

   _____

6. When is the best time for family prayer?

   _____

7. How can we be a witness to God's love?
   a. In our home?_____
   b. In our community?_____

8. In what ways can we serve the poor and the disadvantaged?

   _____

9. What scripture passage reflects our family's mission and purpose?

   _____

10. How can we best deal with problems and difficulties
    in our family?

    _____

STEP 3: PREPARING YOUR FAMILY MISSION STATEMENT

Your **Family Mission Statement** represents a mixture of ideas gained through family discussions and prayer, not a parental proclamation to your children. Through your family's collaboration, everyone's ideas are blended together and poured out into a single cup that will contain a statement of who you are as a family, and what you will accomplish for God.

What makes a good **Family Mission Statement**? It is:

- Brief, defining your family's vision, purpose and desired virtues.

- Clear to all who read it.

- Placed in a prominent location in your home.

- Discussed regularly in family meetings.

As with your **Personal Mission Statement**, your **Family Mission Statement** emphasizes what your family can do in the home, the church and the world. Some opening statements for your **Family Mission Statement** might be:

"In our family, we…"

"In our church, we…"

"In our community, we…"

"As a community of life and love, we are…"

"In the world around us, we will…"

It's important that each member of your family be involved in creating your mission statement. That way, everyone will have ownership of it, including young children and teens.

STEP 4: USING YOUR FAMILY MISSION STATEMENT

Just as with your Personal Mission Statement, assume that your Family Mission Statement is never really "finished." Read it aloud regularly as a family, allowing your children to participate. Have family discussions about how well you're fulfilling your mission, and how you can better align yourselves with your mission statement. Let it serve as your family's "spiritual compass" to help you stay on course to heaven. And don't be afraid to make changes to your mission statement as you seek to make your family everything God wants it to be! Think of it as a "work-in-progress."

Chapter 21

PLAN FOR ACTION

For a car's passengers to arrive at their intended destination, a good deal of navigation and course correction are usually necessary. (Ever try to drive in a straight line without nudging the steering wheel from time to time?) The same is true when you aim for God's will – having a means of measuring your progress and making "course corrections" are needed. **The LifeWork Action Plan Grid** is designed to help you set goals according to God's will and purpose.

It will enable you to create a short- and long-term Action Plan for achieving important goals in the **7 LifeWork Areas**. As you commit to reach these goals, the Action Plan becomes a tool for measuring your progress and holding yourself accountable in listening and accepting the guidance of the Holy Spirit in your life, for following Christ in doing the Father's will – for the wise and holy use of your time. It will also help you identify any course corrections that you need to make along the way.

> **TIP:** It's best to start with your long-term goals (1 year, 5 years), then define shorter-term goals (30 days, 90 days), making sure they contribute to your long-term goals.

THE LIFEWORK ACTION PLAN GRID

FAITH

30 DAYS
90 DAYS
1 YEAR
5 YEARS

RELATIONSHIPS

30 DAYS
90 DAYS
1 YEAR
5 YEARS

WORK

30 DAYS
90 DAYS
1 YEAR
5 YEARS

KNOWLEDGE

30 DAYS
90 DAYS
1 YEAR
5 YEARS

THE LIFEWORK ACTION PLAN GRID

SOCIETY

30 DAYS

90 DAYS

1 YEAR

5 YEARS

FITNESS

30 DAYS

90 DAYS

1 YEAR

5 YEARS

LEISURE

30 DAYS

90 DAYS

1 YEAR

5 YEARS

Chapter 22

WRITE YOUR STORY

Throughout this book, I've asked you to think of our lives as a story being co-authored, co-acted, and co-directed by God and us, as we cooperate with him in living out our unique personal vocation and mission. Naturally, I meant to use "story" as a **word picture**. But have you ever considered actually **writing** your story? That is, physically putting pen to paper and chronicling your spiritual journey? For me, I've found that journaling is an excellent way to focus my thoughts, track my progress and give myself a historic record of my life's journey. And I'd like to encourage you to do the same.

You might ask: Why write? Why can't we just "think" about things and "remember" important events, changes and insights in our lives?

Because we don't.

In our fast-paced world, we tend to zig-zag from one responsibility to the next, frantically trying to keep pace with the many demands made on us. It's rare to have a few quiet minutes at the end of each day to just relax and reflect, let alone write.

Writing helps us refine our thoughts and gives us a reference point for where we've been and where we want to go. It's like taking pictures on a cross-country trip, creating lasting memories of the journey. For years to come, those photographs help us recall people, places and personal experiences. And writing does, too.

There is something unique about our written thoughts. The **visual** nature of them somehow makes them more real... more important. And these notes, if shared with future generations, will give them a uniquely personal and intimate glimpse of ourselves – our lives, our dreams, our struggles and our triumphs.

Life is a Journal

Over the years, I've produced a number of books and videos to help people understand their life-purpose. But by far the most unique of them is ***The LifeWork Principle Journal***. It's unique because most of the book is actually written by the reader! With a guided process and weekly format and plenty of space to write, ***The LifeWork Principle Journal*** can be a valuable tool for helping people listen to and accept the guidance of the Holy Spirit to find, follow and fulfill God's plan for their lives. To follow Christ in doing the Father's will.

Why use ***The LifeWork Principle Journal***? Why not just use a spiral-bound notebook instead? Because this journal is prepared with a structure that helps you **collaborate** with God... to "co-labor" or "work together" with him. By choosing to build your life on rock – cooperating with God and his grace, rather than choosing to build your life on sand – as an individual, private dwelling... you build a strong, secure structure that will withstand the storms of life.

> Through the eyes of faith, you can record the highlights, lowlights and turning points of your life.

Sea captains maintain a logbook to report the events of their journeys. You can think of ***The LifeWork Principle Journal*** as a logbook of your life's journey. But it's also much more than a logbook or personal diary. Here, through the eyes of faith, you can record the highlights, lowlights and turning points of your life as you experience them. You can make journal entries as you pray and read the Bible each day. You can log your thoughts and feelings about key moments in your life. And in the process, you'll gain deep, valuable insight: knowledge about God, yourself and your relationships with others.

Commitment

The process of using **The LifeWork Principle Journal** is more important than the specific results. Why? Because outcomes and "success" are God's business, not ours. Our responsibility is to make our best efforts with the help of God's grace. In your journal, you'll be asked to make commitments each week in the **7 LifeWork Areas.** This will help you adjust your behaviors and activities and point you in the direction of your desired outcomes. Don't worry if you don't achieve those outcomes as quickly as you'd like, or at all. Leave the outcomes to God. Just do your part and trust God to do his… in his way, and in his timing.

To get the most out of **The LifeWork Principle Journal**, go beyond just making journal entries. Consider Bible readings as guidelines for each week – nourishment for your daily prayer life. Take the time to contemplate Christ, to meditate on God's Word in Scripture, and pray each day. Also, read good spiritual books and spend time with other believers, especially in community worship. And visit us at www.lifeworkprinciple.com

The 7 LifeWork Roles

In the story of your life, why accept and live out various roles, responsiblities and personal qualities? To live out our mission and purpose in life more closely, because WHO we are — the quality of our character — greatly impacts WHAT we do in all the **7 LifeWork Areas.** Select a specific role and personal quality each week that will be a particular focus for you, so that you can practice it and turn it into a habit. It helps to think of a person you know or a historical figure that embodies this role and quality. You can change the role and quality each week, or repeat it for as many weeks as you believe necessary.

THE 7 LIFEWORK ROLES

PERSONAL QUALITIES

VISIONARY
- ☐ Creativity
- ☐ Simplicity
- ☐ Influence
- ☐ Purposefulness

OPTIMIST
- ☐ Humor
- ☐ Cheerfulness
- ☐ Joyfulness
- ☐ Hope

COMMUNICATOR
- ☐ Passion
- ☐ Enthusiasm
- ☐ Prayerfulness
- ☐ Honesty

COACH
- ☐ Self-discipline
- ☐ Integrity
- ☐ Perseverance
- ☐ Leadership

FRIEND
- ☐ Trust
- ☐ Tolerance
- ☐ Unselfishness
- ☐ Empathy

PEACEMAKER
- ☐ Forgiveness
- ☐ Respect
- ☐ Patience
- ☐ Calmness

SERVANT
- ☐ Sacrifice
- ☐ Humility
- ☐ Kindness
- ☐ Compassion

Besides the general role of follower (of Christ) and the personal qualities of faith, hope and charity (love), there are others that are worthy of your weekly focus, too. Above are the **7 LifeWork Roles** and their related personal qualities to consider (see the **LifeWork Discovery Process** on page 146 - Preview #5).

Chapter 23

THE LIFEWORK
DISCOVERY PROCESS

As each week comes to an end, take time to look back on the prior week ("review") and look ahead to the coming week ("preview"). Not only can this process help you determine how your life measures up to your **Personal Mission Statement**, it can take you to exciting new levels of personal discovery and discernment! Here's how it works:

REVIEW THE PRIOR WEEK:

1. Pray for guidance of the Holy Spirit.

2. Take a moral inventory of your thoughts, words and actions (good or bad) of the past week.

3. Offer praise and thanksgiving for graces you have received.

4. Offer sorrow for your failings and sins, and ask for God's mercy and forgiveness.

5. Resolve, with the help of God's grace, to avoid sin and strive for moral excellence in the **7 LifeWork Areas.**

PREVIEW THE COMING WEEK:

1. Check your **Personal Mission Statement** for needed adjustments.

2. Think through the coming week in light of the **7 LifeWork Areas.**

3. Set goals and make commitments in the **7 LifeWork Areas.**

4. Ask for the grace to live these commitments.

5. Resolve to follow Christ and live out a particular role and personal quality each week.

Conclusion
THE POSSIBILITIES

Our God is the God of possibilities! We don't know what the future holds, but we know **who** holds the future! We might not know what we're capable of, or what lies around the next corner in the journey of our lives… but he does. After all, he created us as characters in his story! The more we understand that story and our role in it – the Father's unique plan for our lives – the more we'll be able, by his grace, to live to our full potential. Knowing God's plan and following it is the best way to experience an authentic life of lasting peace, joy and fulfillment.

Who will show us that plan and help us to live it? Who will reveal our heavenly Father, his love and his eternal plan for our lives? Who will help us find, follow and fulfill the unique design the Father has prepared for us? The answer is very simple: Jesus. As he tells us in the Gospel: "I am the way, and the truth, and the life" (John 14:6).

Without him, nothing is truly meaningful. But everything changes when we belong to him. In him and by his grace, we are restored – and all things are possible! Just read what the Apostle Paul said about his relationship with Jesus in Philippians 4:13: "I can do all things in him who strengthens me." That is true for us also.

❧ HOW CAN I GET THINGS RIGHT?

As an expert witness in the vocational areas of employability and earning capacity, I often differentiate in court between the "possible" and the "probable." If we allow Jesus to enter our life, **possibilities** become **probabilities** – and **probabilities** become **certainties!** – as he fills our lives with real purpose and direction.

Jesus offers us "true north" in a world that has lost its direction; he sends us the Holy Spirit to direct us; he helps us navigate through the fog of uncertainty, discontent and immorality. And then we experience true freedom, abundant life and amazing love.

The story is often told of a father who had just settled into his easy chair and begun leisurely reading the Sunday newspaper, when his five-year-old son jumped into his lap and asked, "Daddy! Can you play with me?"

> Jesus offers us "true north" in a world that has lost its direction.

The father, knowing he'd never get a moment's peace without giving in, pulled a full-page map of the world from the newspaper. With his wife's sewing scissors, he cut the map into about twenty pieces which he spread across the floor at his feet. He then told his son, "Here's our first game – put together this puzzle of the world, and when you're finished, I'll play with you." Then he returned to his newspaper, confident that it would take his son a long time to put the puzzle together.

But within minutes, his son announced, "Daddy, I finished the puzzle!" Amazed, the father looked to the floor, and sure enough, the puzzle was complete. "How did you put it together so fast?" the stunned father asked.

"It was easy, Daddy," the five-year-old answered. "On the back of the map, there was a picture of a man. I put the man together first, and when I did that, the whole world fit right into place."

The lesson? When you get the man right, you get the world right. Put Jesus first in your life, and your world will make a lot more sense.

Jesus is the Master Craftsman in the Father's workshop of human life! It is the trade he knows best. And we can choose to be his apprentices. He will never fail us or let us down:

Jesus will LEAD us in prayer. He sends the Holy Spirit to guide us in how to pray, often using silence as his classroom, so that we can better hear God's call. We can learn how to go beyond asking for God's help in our needs, as we contemplate Christ in the Bible, seek forgiveness and offer thanksgiving and praise.

Jesus will TEACH us what there is to learn about life – such as authentic love and mercy, purity of body, mind and spirit, the value of simplicity and personal responsibility.

Jesus will GUIDE us in and through every situation, event and relationship – in the good times and the bad. He will be there when we need him and will watch over us. We can turn to him with trust in our needs.

Jesus will EQUIP us with the skills and the virtues that help us get through life. He knows what we need. If we just ask him, he will see that our needs are met abundantly.

Jesus will PROTECT us from sin and Satan. Our primary opponents in this life are the world, the flesh and the devil; Jesus has overcome them and will help us to do so also.

Jesus will WORK in us and with us, side-by-side – not just in our job, but in all the **7 LifeWork Areas** that comprise our LifeWork: in all the settings in which we find ourselves. Guided by the Holy Spirit, we can use our talents and skills as our way of fulfilling the Father's will. Our LifeWork, then, becomes an expression of our love that brings glory to God, when we use those talents and skills in the home, the workplace, the church and the world.

Jesus will HELP us achieve those virtues that place us on high moral ground, far above the worldly pursuit or promotion of "self;" seeking true **purpose**, not pleasure. When we belong to Christ through baptism, we receive from him the fundamental virtues we need in life: faith, hope and charity.

That's the Jesus I know. And that's the Jesus we know from the Bible. My prayer is that you will fully embrace the abundant life and the many blessings and graces that flow from him.

> *Let him* LEAD *you to the Father.*
>
> *Let him* TEACH *you about virtues.*
>
> *Let him* GUIDE *you through life.*
>
> *Let him* EQUIP *you with the skills you need.*
>
> *Let him* PROTECT *you from evil.*
>
> *Let him* WORK *with you in self-giving love.*
>
> *Let him* HELP *you in all the difficulties and struggles of life.*

Even though you've nearly completed this book, you really aren't finishing anything here. In fact, when you arrived at this section, you arrived at a **starting** point for a lifetime of joy, meaning and satisfaction!

If you began this book with doubt, depression or even despair, I hope you're concluding it with **hope** and **purpose**.

If you began this book seeking the path to deeper satisfaction and meaning, I hope you're concluding it with a **personal plan** in place.

If you began this book by just "considering" that God exists, I hope you're concluding it with the **certainty** that God loves you and desires a closer, personal relationship with you.

In other words, I hope your life has changed! You are a unique, unrepeatable work of God, and an essential part of the Father's eternal plan in Christ. You are now equipped to explore your life-purpose through the **daily process** of discovery.

As you close this book, I want to encourage you to continue the journey you've made thus far. To do this, I recommend that you read daily from God's Word, the Bible. As I mentioned earlier, a great place to begin is with the Gospels: Matthew, Mark, Luke or John. (The word "Gospel," by the way, means "good news" – and in these books, you'll discover exactly why the life, death and resurrection of Jesus is the best news humanity has ever received!)

I'd also like to encourage you to pray. If you've never prayed before, rest assured, there's really no "wrong way" to do it – simply open your heart to God and begin an internal dialogue with him. No relationship can grow without communication. Reading God's Word and personal prayer opens the lines of communication between you and your creator. There is no greater relationship you can enter than this one!

Third, get involved in a church in your community, where you'll find caring Christians who can give you the answers and support you need for your life's journey. Living according to God's purpose isn't always easy – he never promised it would be – and it's helpful to surround yourself with other believers who can help bear your burdens and give you strength and encouragement as you grow in your faith.

You and I are both characters in God's amazing story, and I'm glad the author has allowed our "storylines" to intersect in this way. I hope you're as encouraged as I am. Now, let's pray that you and I will put these ideas into **action**… making every moment of our lives count for time and eternity… making sure we stay on course, following Christ on the journey to our Father in heaven. May the story of our lives take us to new, unexplored territories of true joy and purpose!

Afterword

Finding your true purpose, deep personal fulfillment and real joy begins when you change your perspective on life and take action. But ultimately, it depends on your willingness to *trust* – to place your life in the hands of the God who created you, and trust him to carry you through the peaks and valleys of your daily existence.

That kind of trust was powerfully illustrated on August 17, 1859, by a daredevil named Charles Blondin, known worldwide as the most gifted tightrope walker of his generation. On that August day, hundreds of thousands of people gathered to witness the most spectacular and dangerous attempt of his career: crossing Niagara Falls on a 3-inch hemp cord stretching 1,100 feet across the falls, anchored 160 feet above the water at one side, and 270 feet at the other.

Ever the showman, Blondin stepped onto the cord and hushed the roaring crowd with a question: "Do you believe I can carry someone on my back across the falls?"

Without hesitation, the audience responded as one voice, "We believe! We believe!"

Then Blondin asked, "Who would like to be that someone?" But suddenly the only response was embarrassed silence. He pointed to various people, asking each if they would be willing to climb on his back as he crossed the falls, always with the same answer: "No."

Ultimately, it was Blondin's manager, Harry Colcord, who agreed to ride the daredevil's back. Maybe he felt that since he profited from Blondin's risky endeavors, he ought to demonstrate his trust in a tangible way. Or perhaps Colcord simply wanted to ensure that the audience enjoyed a more dramatic show. But he put his trust into action, and nervously climbed on Blondin's back for the crossing.

Step by step, Blondin and his manager made their way across the gorge. Since Colcord was taller and heavier than Blondin, they had to stop at regular intervals for Blondin to rest. During one such stop, Blondin instructed his manager not to try to balance himself as they crossed – to let Blondin balance the two of them.

"If you do anything on your own, we will both die," Blondin said.

Colcord climbed again onto the daredevil's back, and the two safely completed their crossing of Niagara Falls – a harrowing journey that lasted an agonizing 42 minutes.

Harry Colcord proved his trust in Charles Blondin by placing his life in the hands of his client – a mere human being, who could make mistakes. But God is infinitely more trustworthy than any man. Are we willing to give God more than just lip-service? Are we ready to really trust him – and put our faith into action?

The Bible puts it this way: "Faith by itself, if it has no works, is dead" (James 2:17).

Do all you can to keep your faith from withering because of underuse. If these pages have brought you to the point of trusting in God, demonstrate that trust by giving your life over to him – your entire life – the good, the bad and the downright ugly. And watch God do something far more amazing with it than just carrying it on a tightrope!

Each of us has been given the gift of *freedom* – freedom to choose and to act. In this book, I have advocated a creative *collaboration* between you and God. If you are still open to the message of this book, then let me encourage you with three key steps that, with God's grace, can help you to implement the ideas we've covered:

1. REFER to your **Personal Mission Statement** weekly. Are you staying on course?

2. GO through the **LifeWork Discovery Process** on a weekly basis, reviewing your past week and looking ahead to the coming week. Any course corrections you need to make?

3. USE *The LifeWork Principle Journal* as the written record of working the weekly process. Are you including your personal and spiritual insights?

The key to all of this is *consistency*. Week-by-week, page-by-page, you will see how an authentic partnership with Christ leads you to true fulfillment in life. We're talking about real results, in both time *and* eternity. I hope these ideas, this book and this ongoing process brings you true happiness, abundant joy and great peace!

Rick Sarkisian